HOUSE OF BLUES

Presents

BLUES GUITAR COURSE BOOK
EXPANDED EDITION

Written & Method By:
John McCarthy

Adapted By: Jimmy Rutkowski
Supervising Editor: Joe Palombo
Music Transcribing & Engraving: Jimmy Rutkowski
Production Manager: Joe Palombo
Layout, Graphics & Design: Jimmy Rutkowski
Photography: Jimmy Rutkowski, Rodney Dabney
Copy Editors: Cathy McCarthy, Alex Palombo

Cover Art Direction & Design:
Jimmy Rutkowski

HL14041784
ISBN: 978-1-4584-5968-8
Produced by The Rock House Method®
© 2012 Fred Russell Publishing, LLC All Rights Reserved

Table of Contents

About the Author 5
Introduction 6
Icon Key 7

Chapter 1 8
Essential Blues Tools 8
Tuning 9
Parts of the Guitar 10
Reading a Chord Chart 11
Open Blues Chords 12
    Open Major Chords 12
    Open Minor Chords 14
Open Chord Blues 16
    Major Blues 16
    Minor Blues 17
    Rhythm Notation 18
Tablature Explanation 19
Blues 20

Chapter 2 22
The Minor Pentatonic Scale 22
    1st Position A Minor Pentatonic Scale 22
    2nd Position A Minor Pentatonic Scale 22
    3rd Position A Minor Pentatonic Scale 23
    4th Position A Minor Pentatonic Scale 23
    5th Position A Minor Pentatonic Scale 23
    Minor Pentatonic Scale Fretboard Diagram 24
    Alternate Picking 24
Lead Patterns 25
    Double Lead Pattern 25
    Triplet Lead Pattern 26
Lead Techniques 28
    Bending 28
    Hammer Ons 29
    Pull Offs 29
Complete Blues Lead 30

Chapter 3 31
Creating a Great Blues Sound 31
Blues Riffs That Will Make Yo Mama Scream 32
The B.B. Box 34
Shuffle Blues Rhythm 35
Full Blues Lead 36

Chapter 4 38
- Barre Chords 38
  - 6th String Barre Chords 38
  - 5th String Barre Chords 40
- Understanding the 12 Bar Blues Concept 42
- Single Note Blues Rhythm 43
  - Transposing the Minor Pentatonic Scale 44

Chapter 5 45
- Lead Techniques 45
  - Slides 45
  - Vibrato 45
- Rockin' the Blues - Dead Strums 46
- Blues Riffs That Will Make Yo Mama Scream Part 2 46
- Open Chord Blues Progression in Em 48

Chapter 6 50
- Blues Scales - Key of E 50
  - 1st Position E Blues Scale 50
  - 2nd Position E Blues Scale 50
  - 3rd Position E Blues Scale 51
  - 4th Position E Blues Scale 51
  - 5th Position E Blues Scale 51
  - Open Position E Blues Scale 52
  - Blues Scale Fretboard Diagram 52
- Open String Blues Rhythm in E 53
- Advanced Bending Techniques 54
  - Half Step Bend 54
  - Ghost Bend 54
  - Double Pump Bend 54
  - Scream Bend 54
- Blues Lead in E 55

Chapter 7 56
- Open Chords 56
  - Major Chords 56
  - Minor Chords 56
- Advanced Blues Jazz Chords 57
- The Jazz Blues Fuze 60
- Lead Techniques 61
  - Rakes 61
  - Pick & Finger 62
- Advanced Blues Riffs 63

Chapter 8 66
- Barre Chords 66
    - 6th String Barre Chords 66
    - 5th String Barre Chords 66
- Skipping Strings 67
- The C Major Pentatonic Scale 68
    - 1st Position C Major Pentatonic Scale 68
    - 2nd Position C Major Pentatonic Scale 68
    - 3rd Position C Major Pentatonic Scale 69
    - 4th Position C Major Pentatonic Scale 69
    - 5th Position C Major Pentatonic Scale 69
- Fast Blues in C (Sliding Rhythm) 70
- Combining Major and Minor Scales 72
- Improvisation Exercise 73

Chapter 9 74
- Sixteenth Note Lead Pattern 74
    - 1st Position D Minor Pentatonic 74
    - 2nd Position D Minor Pentatonic 75
- Blues Rock Progression - Key of D 76
- Classic Old School Blues Turnarounds 78

Chapter 10 80
- Modern Blues Progression - Circle of Fourths 80
- Natural Minor Scales 81
    - 1st Position A Minor Scale 81
    - 2nd Position A Minor Scale 81
    - Melodic Lead 82
- Slide Technique and Rhythm 83
- E Blues Riff Rhythm 84
- E Blues Solo 85

Chord Glossary 87

Circle of 4ths and 5ths 90

All Keys Relative Minor 91

Scale Glossary 92

Never Coming Back 96

Changing a String 99

House of Blues 101

Backing Track List & Index 103

About the Author

John McCarthy
Creator of
the Rock House Method

John is the creator of **The Rock House Method**®, the world's leading musical instruction system. Over his 20 year career, he has produced and/or appeared in more than 100 instructional products. Millions of people around the world have learned to play music using John's easy to follow, accelerated program.

John is a virtuoso guitarist who has worked with some of the industry's most legendary musicians. He has the ability to break down, teach and communicate music in a manner that motivates and inspires others to achieve their dreams of playing an instrument.

As a guitarist and songwriter, John blends together a unique style of Rock, Metal, Funk and Blues in a collage of melodic compositions, jam-packed with masterful guitar techniques. His sound has been described as a combination of vintage guitar rock with a progressive, gritty edge that is perfectly suited for today's audiences.

Throughout his career, John has recorded and performed with renowned musicians like Doug Wimbish (who has worked with Joe Satriani, Living Colour, The Rolling Stones, Madonna, Annie Lennox and many more top flight artists), Grammy winner Leo Nocentelli, Rock & Roll Hall of Fame inductees Bernie Worrell and Jerome "Big Foot" Brailey, Freekbass, Gary Hoey, Bobby Kimball, David Ellefson (founding member of seven time Grammy nominee Megadeth), Will Calhoun (who has worked with B.B. King, Mick Jagger and Paul Simon), Jordan Giangreco from the acclaimed band The Breakfast, and solo artist Alex Bach. John has also shared the stage with Blue Oyster Cult, Randy Bachman, Marc Rizzo, Jerry Donahue, Bernard Fowler, Stevie Salas, Brian Tichy, Kansas, Al Dimeola and Dee Snyder.

For more information on John, his music and his instructional products visit www.rockhousemethod.com.

The Rock House Method

CREATING MUSICIANS ONE LESSON AT A TIME

Introduction

Welcome to **The Rock House Method®** system of learning. You are joining millions of aspiring musicians around the world who use our easy-to-understand methods for learning to play music.

Unlike conventional learning programs, The Rock House Method® is a four-part teaching system that employs DVD, backing tracks and 24/7 online lesson support along with this book to give you a variety of sources to assure a complete learning experience. The products can be used individually or together. The DVD's that come with this book match the curriculum exactly, providing you with a live instructor for visual reference. In addition, the DVD's contain some valuable extras like sections on changing your strings, guitar care and an interactive chord library.

How to Use the Lesson Support Site

Every Rock House product offers FREE membership to our interactive *Lesson Support* site. Use the member number included with your book to register at www.rockhousemethod.com. You will find your member number on the sleeve that contains your DVD's. Once registered, you can use this fully interactive site along with your product to enhance your learning experience, expand your knowledge, link with instructors, and connect with a community of people around the world who are learning to play music using The Rock House Method®. There are sections that directly correspond to this product within the Additional Information and Backing Tracks sections. There are also a variety of other tools you can utilize such as Ask The Teacher, Quizzes, Reference Material, Definitions, Forums, Live Chats, Guitar Professor and much more.

Icon Key

Throughout this book, you'll periodically notice the following icons. They indicate when there are additional learning tools available on our support website for the section you're working on. When you see an icon in the book, visit the member section of www.rockhousemethod.com for musical backing tracks, additional information and learning utilities.

Backing Track Number

There are accompanying backing tracks and audio demonstrations available for you to download from the *Lesson Support* site at www.rockhousemethod.com. When you see this backing track icon in the book note the track number that will correspond with the lesson. We have divided the tracks into two audio CD partitions as recommended for burning onto disc.

Additional Information

The question mark icon indicates there is more information for that section available on the website. It can be theory, more playing examples, or tips.

Metronome

Metronome icons are placed next to the examples that we recommend you practice using a metronome. You can download a free, adjustable metronome from our support site.

Tablature

This icon indicates that there is additional guitar tablature available on the website that corresponds to the lesson. There is also an extensive database of music online that is updated regularly.

Tuner

Also found on the website is a free online tuner that you can use to help you tune your instrument.

CHAPTER 1

Essential Blues Tools

Solid Body Electric Guitar

The solid body electric is the standard electric guitar that's great for distortion sounds and lead playing. Pickups mounted on the guitar's body send the sound to an amplifier. If there are two (or more) pickups, a pickup selector switch (*toggle switch*) is used to select one or blend them together. Pickups located near the bridge (*bridge pickups*) tend to have a brighter sound, making them better suited for lead playing. Pickups closer to the neck (*neck pickups*) have a warmer sound, making them a good choice for rhythm playing. A humbucker pickup is a popular double coil pickup designed to cancel electronic hum.

Acoustic Guitar

An acoustic guitar is an ideal choice for intimate performances, classic blues, fingerpicking, country, or bluegrass. The sound is projected out from the body of the guitar through the sound hole, making an amplifier unnecessary. An acoustic/electric is a type of acoustic guitar with built in pickups, allowing it to be amplified through an amp or PA system.

Hollow Body Electric Guitar

A hollow body electric guitar is a hybrid of the regular acoustic and electric guitars. It has F-holes on the front of the body, allowing the sound to resonate. These guitars are the choice of many classic blues and slide guitarists.

Picks

There are many different types of picks in different thicknesses. A heavy pick may offer you more control for lead playing, but medium and light picks have a flexibility that's good for rhythm playing.

Strings

Strings are available in different gauges. Heavier gauge strings produce a thicker, fuller sound; lighter gauges are thinner, easier to bend, and great for soloing.

Tuning

Each of the six strings on a guitar is tuned to and named after a different note (*pitch*). The thinnest or 1st string is referred to as the highest string because it is the *highest sounding* string. The thickest or 6th string is referred to as the lowest string because it is the *lowest sounding* string. Memorize the names of the open strings. These notes form the basis for finding any other notes on the guitar.

Names of the Open Strings

6th string	5th string	4th string	3rd string	2nd string	1st string
E	A	D	G	B	E

6th string (thickest) lowest sounding string

1st string (thinnest) highest sounding string

Tune your guitar using the machine heads on the headstock. Turn the machine heads a little bit at a time while plucking the string and listening to the change in pitch. Tighten the string to raise the pitch. Loosen the string to lower the pitch. Be careful not to accidentally break a string by tightening it too much or too quickly.

The easiest way to tune a guitar is to use an electronic tuner. There are many different kinds available that are fairly inexpensive. You can also download the free online tuner from www.rockhousemethod.com.

Parts of the Guitar

The guitar is divided into three main sections: the body, the neck and the headstock. The guitar's input jack will be located on the side or front of the body. The assembly that anchors the strings to the body is called the bridge. The saddles hold the strings properly in place; the height of each string (or *action*) can be adjusted with the saddle. Mounted to the body behind the strings are the pickups. A pickup functions like the guitar's microphone; it picks up the vibrations of the strings and converts them to a signal that travels through the guitar cord to the amplifier. Also located on the front of the body are the volume and tone knobs and the pickup selector switch or *toggle switch*. Strap buttons are located on both sides of the body where a guitar strap can be attached. The front face of the neck is called the fretboard (or *fingerboard*). The metal bars going across the fretboard are called frets. The dots are position markers (or *fret markers*) for visual reference to help you gauge where you are on the neck while playing. The nut is the string guide that holds the strings in place where the neck meets the headstock. The headstock contains the machine heads (also referred to as *tuners*); the machine heads are used to tune the strings by tightening or loosening them.

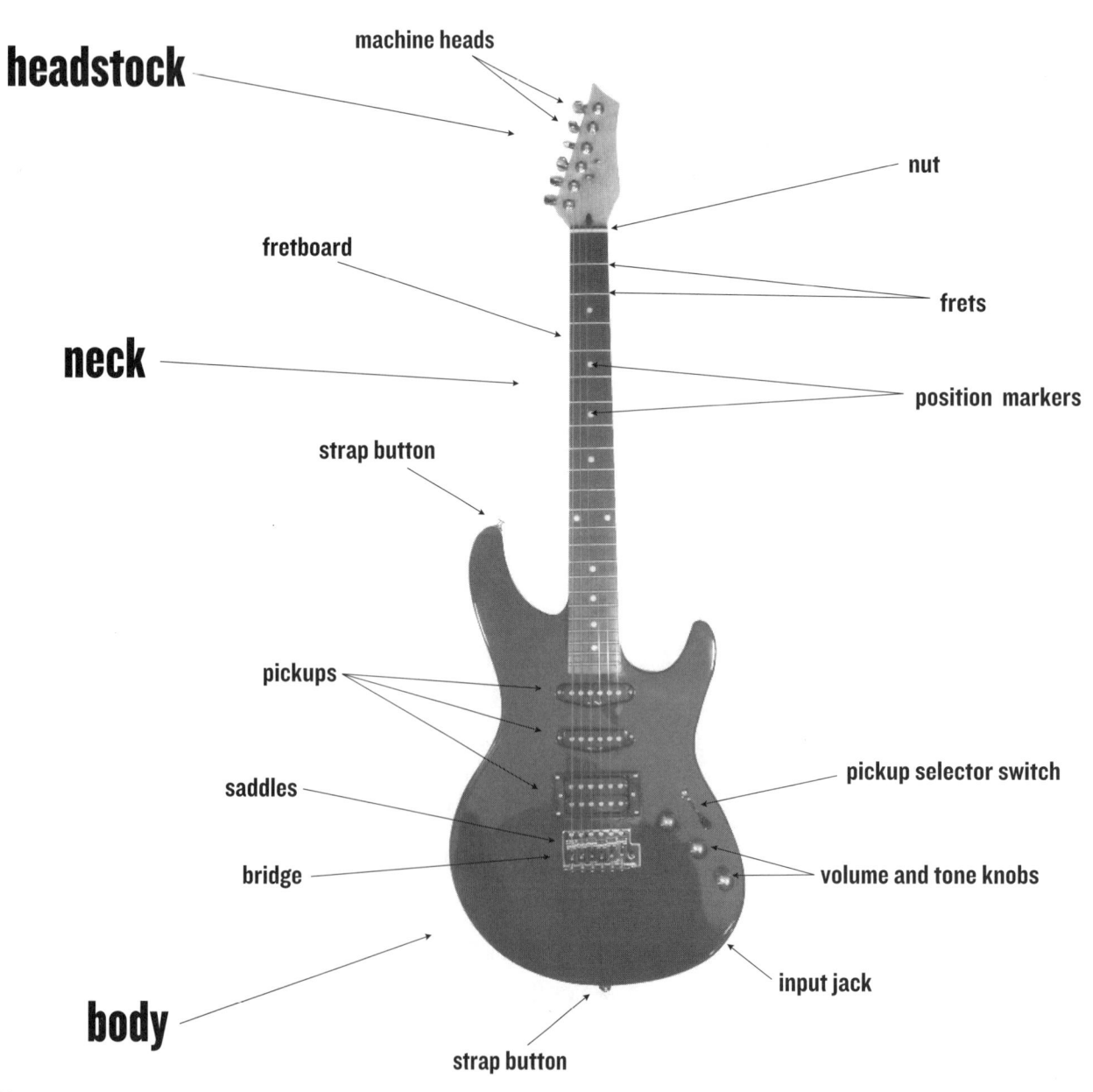

Reading a Chord Chart

A chord chart (*chord diagram*) is a graphic representation of part of the fretboard (as if you stood the guitar up from floor to ceiling and looked directly at the front of the neck). The vertical lines represent the strings; the horizontal lines represent the frets.

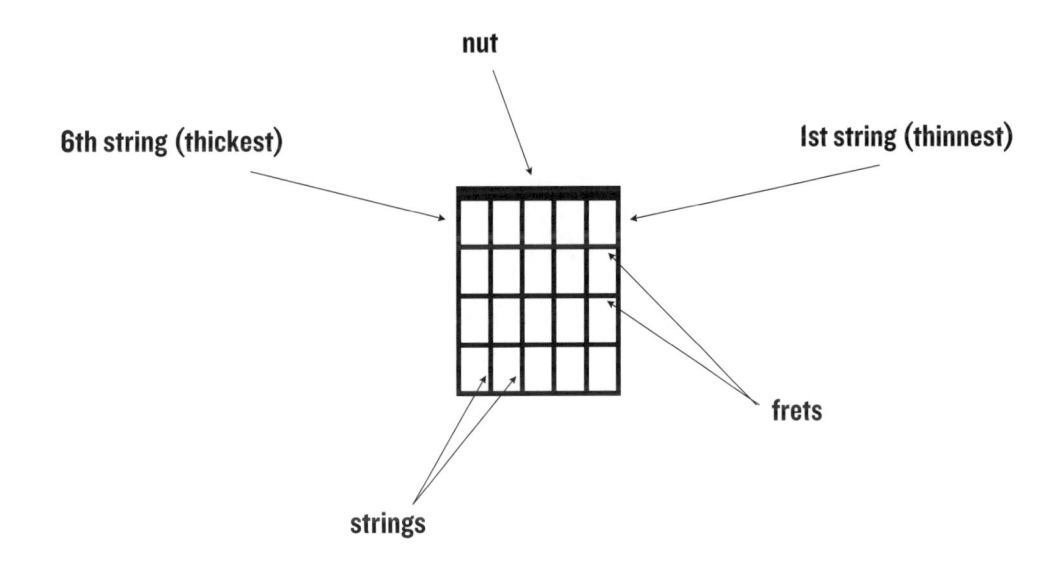

Chord diagrams show which notes to play and which strings they are played on. The solid black dots within the graph represent fretted notes and show you where your fingers should go. Each of these dots will have a number directly below it, underneath the diagram. These numbers indicate which left hand finger to fret the note with (1 = index, 2 = middle, 3 = ring, 4 = pinky). The 0s at the bottom of the diagram show which strings are played open (strummed with no left hand fingers touching them).

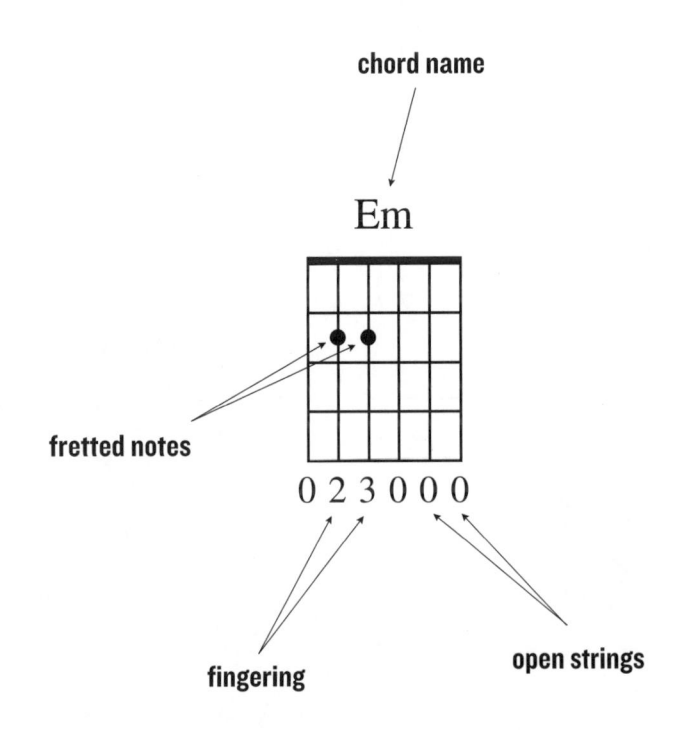

Open Blues Chords

Open Major Chords

The following open major chords are the most commonly used in rock and blues progressions. These three chords, **A**, **D**, and **E**, represent the **I - IV - V** (*one - four - five*) chords in the key of A major. The roman numerals refer to the steps of the scale, relative to what key the music is in. The A chord is the **I** chord (also called the *tonic*). The D chord is the **IV** chord (also called the *subdominant*) because in the key of A, D is the fourth step of the scale. Finally, the **V** chord (or *dominant*) is the E chord, because E is the fifth step of the scale in the key of A. To find the I - IV - V chords in any key, build chords on the 1st, 4th and 5th degrees of the scale.

The I - IV - V chord progression is the foundation that all rock and blues was built on and has evolved from. There are many variations, but songs such as "Johnny B. Goode," "You Really Got Me," "Rock and Roll," "I Love Rock and Roll" and "Sympathy for the Devil" are all based on the I - IV - V.

In the **A** chord diagram, the slur going across the notes means you should *barre* (bar) those notes. A barre is executed by placing one finger flat across more than one string. Pick each note of the chord individually to make sure you're applying enough pressure with your finger. Notice that the 6th and 1st strings each have an "x" below them on the diagram, indicating these strings are not played (either muted or not strummed). For each chord, the first photo shows what the chord looks like from the front. The second photo is from the player's perspective.

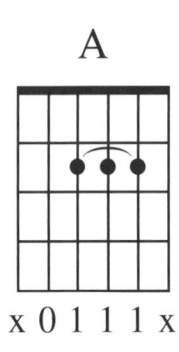

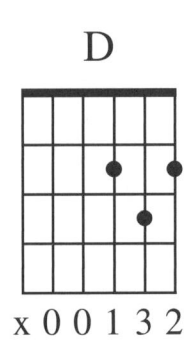

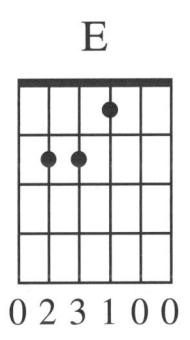

D

x 0 0 1 3 2

E

0 2 3 1 0 0

Open Minor Chords

Here are the I - IV - V chords in the key of A minor: **Am**, **Dm** and **Em**. Minor chords have a sad or melancholy sound, whereas the major chords have a bright or happy sound.

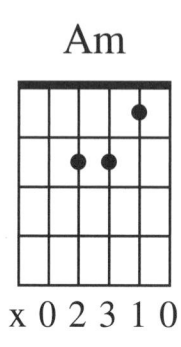

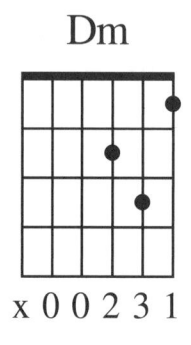

Am

x 0 2 3 1 0

Dm

x 0 0 2 3 1

14

Em

0 2 3 0 0 0

Be sure to use proper left hand technique when playing chords for maximum tone and control. Remember to keep your thumb firmly anchored against the back of the neck. Your fingers should be curled inward toward the fretboard and only the tips of your fingers should be touching the strings. Don't grab the neck with your whole hand; no other parts of your fingers or hand should be touching the neck or any of the other strings. Place your fingertips just to the left of (behind) the fret, pressing the strings inward toward the neck. When strumming chords, pivot from your elbow and keep your wrist straight; the strumming motion should come from your elbow and wrist. When playing single notes, use more wrist.

One of the hardest things for a beginner to conquer is the ability to play a clean, fully sustained chord without buzzing strings, muted or dead notes. Make sure your left hand is fretting the proper notes and your fingers aren't accidentally touching any of the other strings. Pick each string individually with your right hand, one note at a time. If any of the open strings are deadened or muted, try *slightly* adjusting your fingers. If any of the fretted notes are buzzing, you probably aren't pressing down hard enough with your fingers. It will be difficult at first and might hurt a little, but don't get discouraged. With time and practice, you'll build up callouses on your fingertips. Before you know it, playing chords will be second nature and your fingers will hardly feel it at all.

Once you have the chords sounding clean and the strumming motion down, the next step is to learn how to change chords quickly and cleanly. Focus on where each finger needs to move for the next chord. Sometimes one or more of your fingers will be able to stay in the same place. Avoid taking your hand completely off the neck. Instead, try to move your whole hand as little as possible and make smaller finger adjustments to change from one chord to the next. When you can change from chord to chord seamlessly, you'll be able to play complete songs.

Open Chord Blues

The following is an example of a *chord progression* and is written on a musical *staff*. A staff is the group of horizontal lines on which music is written. The chord names above the staff show which chord to play, and the *rhythm slashes* indicate the rhythm in which the chords are strummed. In this chord progression, strum each chord twice, using all downstrums. This example also uses *repeat signs* (play through the progression and repeat it again). Listen and play along with the backing track to hear how it should sound. Keep practicing and try to change chords in time without stalling or missing a beat. Count along out loud with each strum, in time and on the beat. Start out slowly if you need to and gradually get it up to speed.

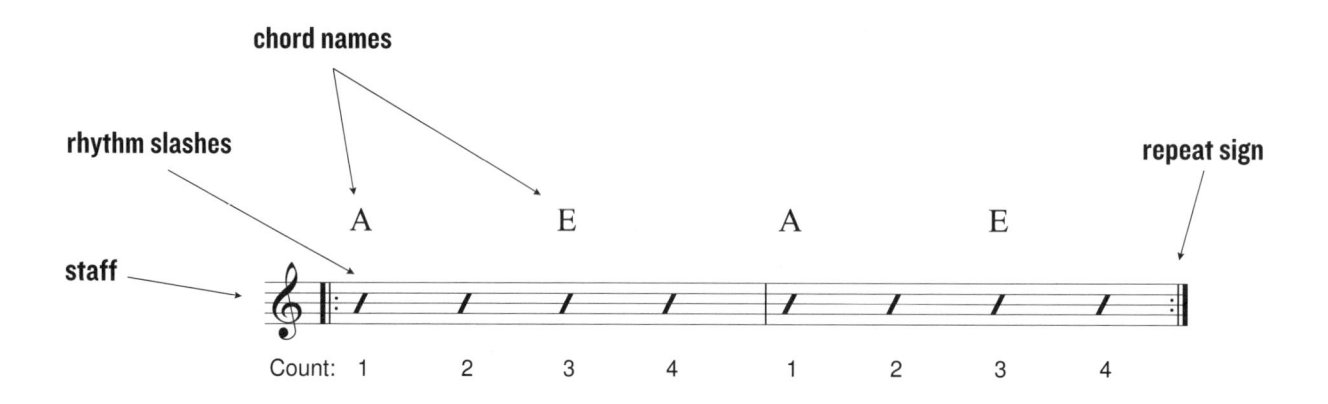

Major Blues

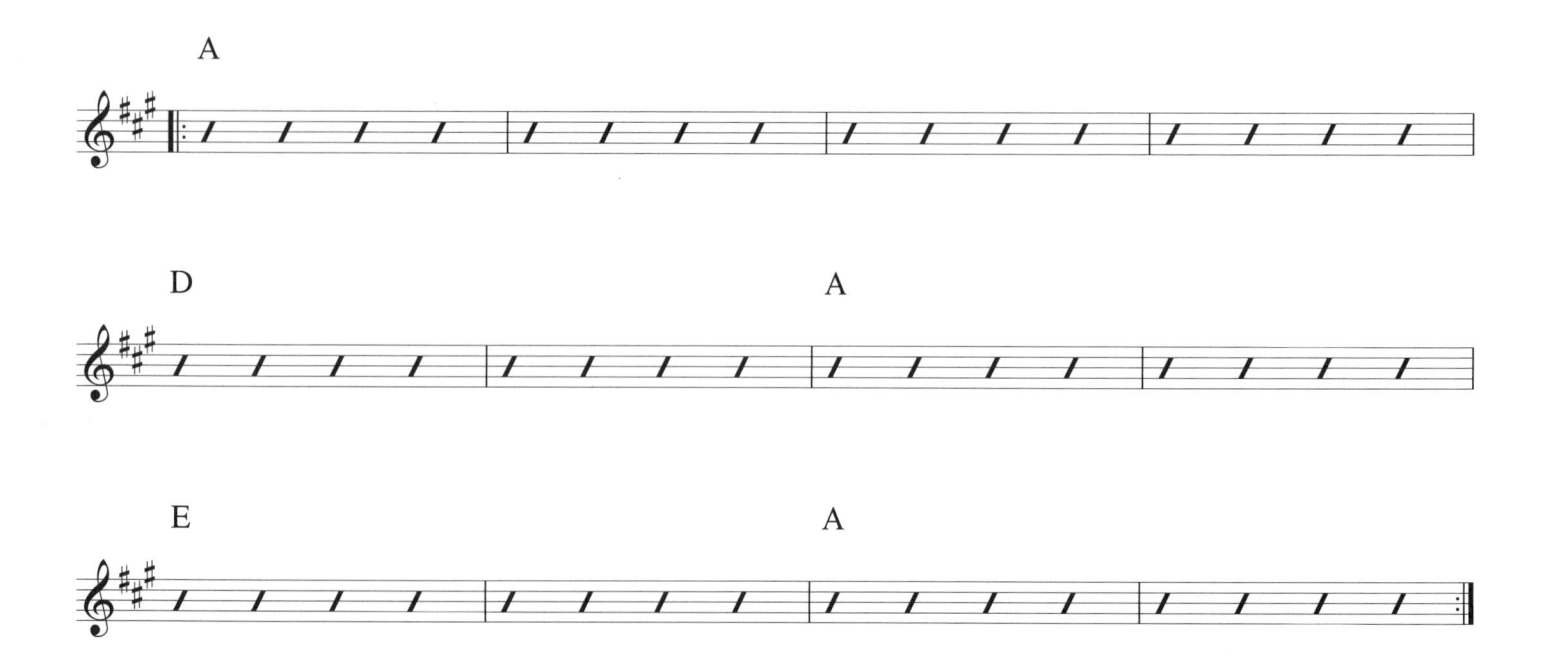

Minor Blues

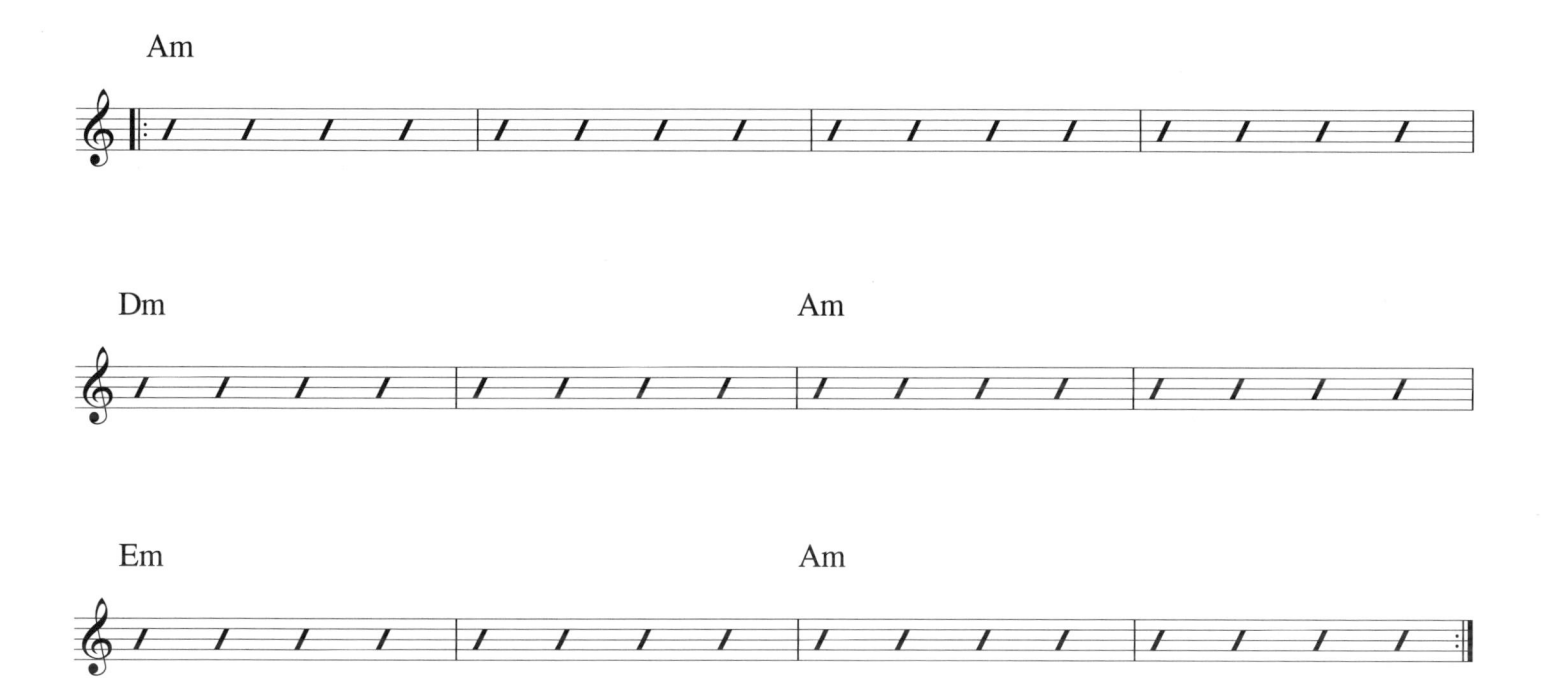

Am

Dm   Am

Em   Am

Quick Tip!

MAKE SURE YOUR GUITAR IS SET UP PROPERLY

Beginners don't usually realize that their new guitar may need to be set up for it to play comfortably. A proper set up will ensure that the strings are at the correct height. If they're too high off the neck, it will be harder to press the strings down. You'll also want to check the neck adjustment to be sure your guitar neck has the proper curve. Even right out of the box, new guitars need adjusting. This oversight can cause many beginners to give up in frustration before giving it a fair chance on a properly adjusted instrument.

Rhythm Notation

You don't need to read traditional music notation in order to play guitar, but it's helpful to understand a little bit about the concept of rhythm and timing. In most popular rock and blues, music is divided into *measures* of four beats. When a band counts off "One, two, three, four" at the beginning of a song, it represents one complete measure of music. Different types of notes are held for different durations within a measure. For example, a *quarter note* gets one beat because a quarter note is held for one quarter of a measure.

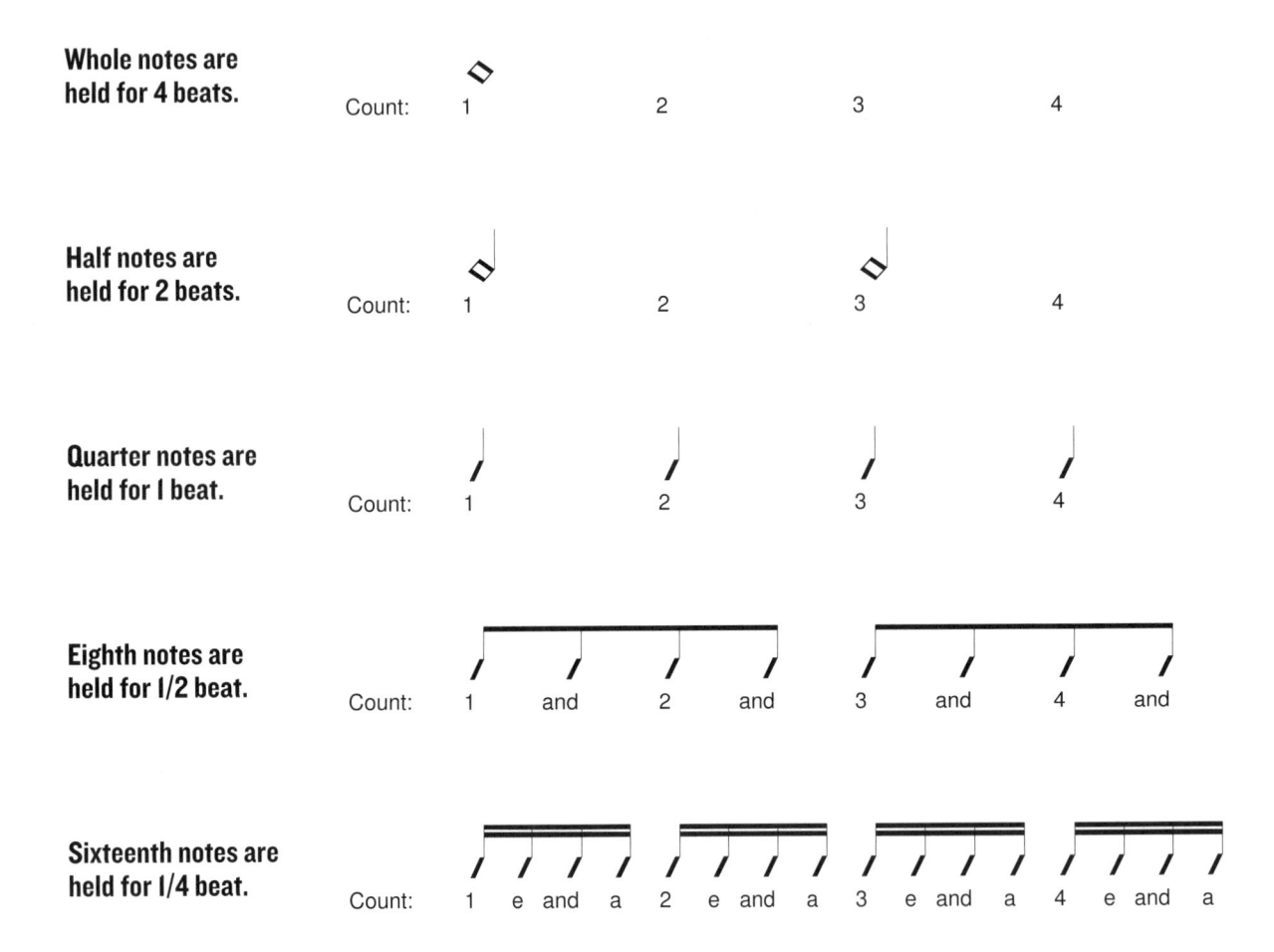

Whole notes are held for 4 beats.
Count: 1   2   3   4

Half notes are held for 2 beats.
Count: 1   2   3   4

Quarter notes are held for 1 beat.
Count: 1   2   3   4

Eighth notes are held for 1/2 beat.
Count: 1 and 2 and 3 and 4 and

Sixteenth notes are held for 1/4 beat.
Count: 1 e and a 2 e and a 3 e and a 4 e and a

A *tie* is a curved line connecting one note to the next. If two notes are tied, strike only the first one and let it ring out through the duration of the second note (or "tied" note).

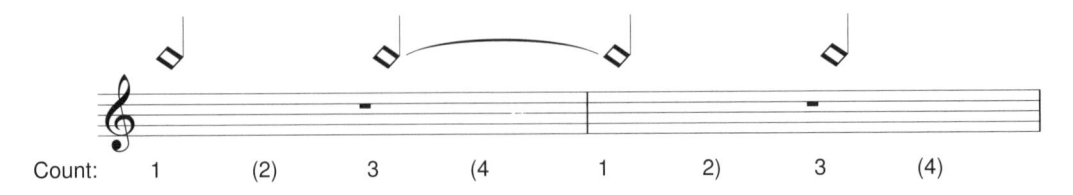

Count: 1 (2) 3 (4   1 2) 3 (4)

A *dot* after a note increases its value by another 1/2 of its original value. In the following example the half notes are dotted, so they are held for three beats.

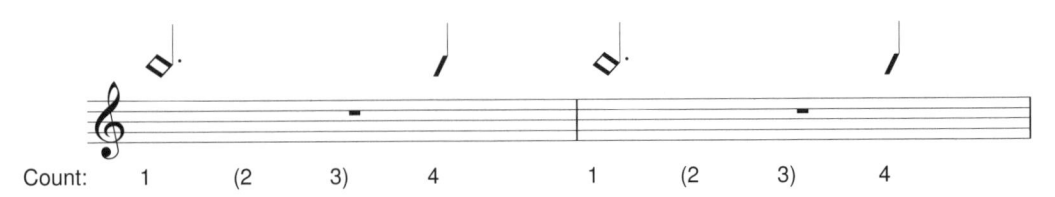

Count: 1 (2 3) 4   1 (2 3) 4

Tablature Explanation

Tablature (or *tab*) is a number system for reading notes on the neck of a guitar. It does not require you to have knowledge of standard music notation. This system was designed specifically for the guitar. Most music for guitar is available in tab. Tablature is a crucial and essential part of your guitar playing career.

The six lines of the tablature staff represent each of the six strings. The top line is the thinnest (highest pitched) string. The bottom line is the thickest (lowest pitched) string. The lines in between are the 2nd through 5th strings. The numbers placed directly on these lines show you the fret number to play the note at. At the bottom, underneath the staff, is a series of numbers. These numbers show you which left hand fingers you should use to fret the notes.

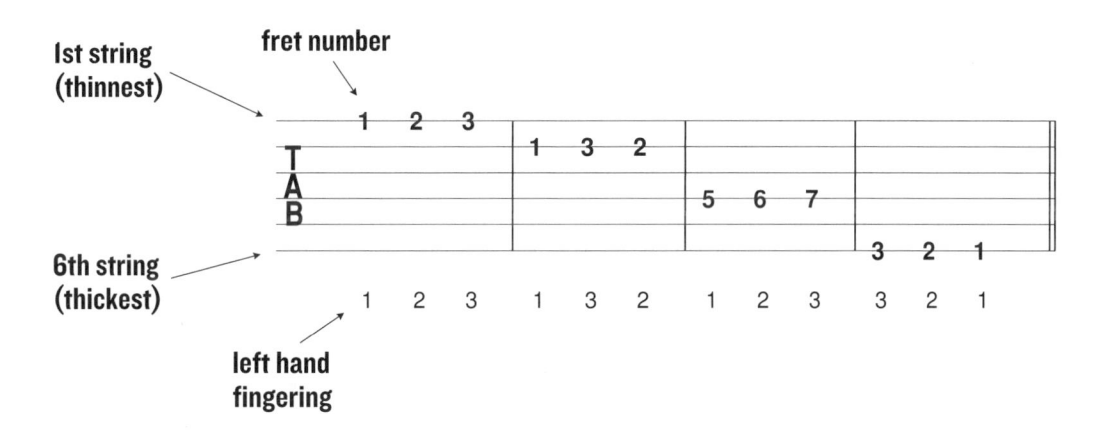

Chords can also be written in tab. If there are several numbers stacked together in a column, those notes should be played or strummed at the same time. Here are the chords you've already learned with the tablature written out underneath each diagram. Since the fingerings are shown on the chord diagrams, we won't bother to repeat them underneath the tab.

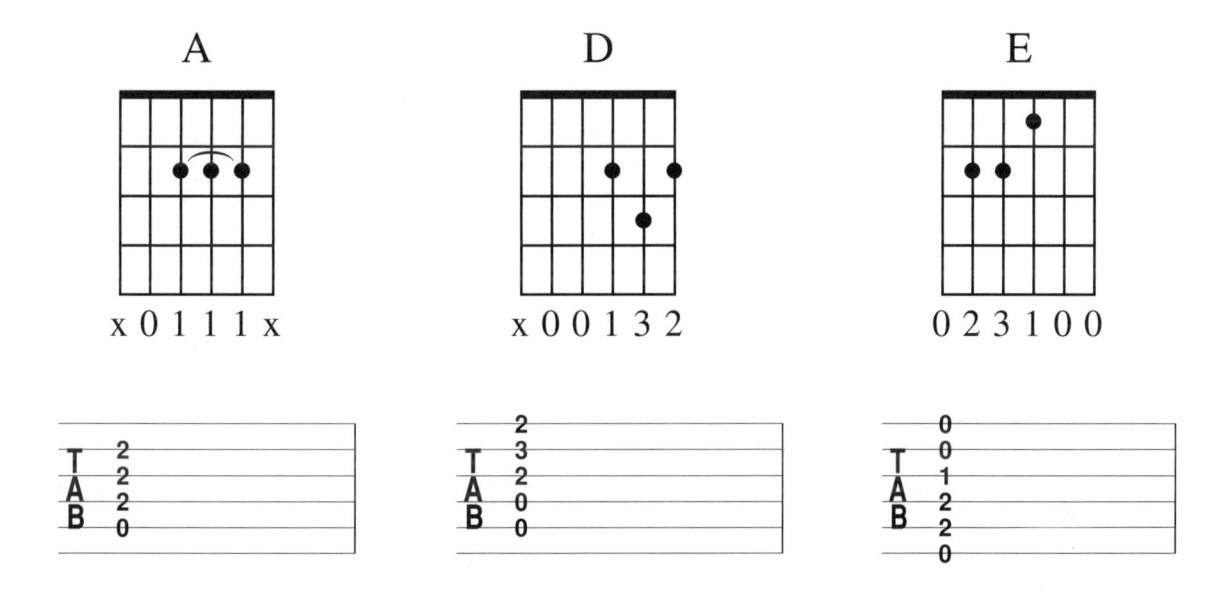

A
x 0 1 1 1 x

D
x 0 0 1 3 2

E
0 2 3 1 0 0

19

Am
x 0 2 3 1 0

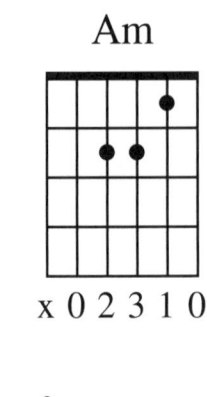

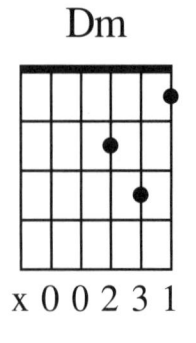

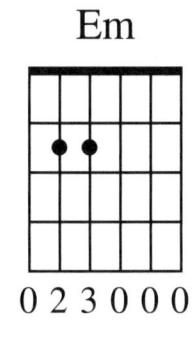

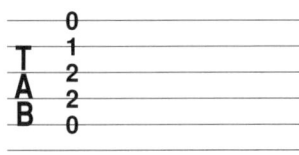

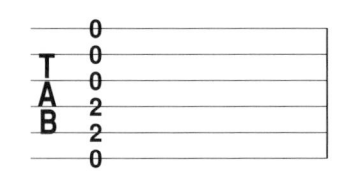

Dm
x 0 0 2 3 1

Em
0 2 3 0 0 0

Blues

The following is a basic blues riff in the key of A. This riff is made up of two note chords shown on the tab staff. The chord names above the staff are there as a reference to show you what the basic harmony is while you play along.

This riff should sound very familiar - it's used more than any other blues progression. Plenty of rock and blues classics are played entirely with this one riff repeated over and over. It is made up of 12 measures (or *bars*) of music, called the *12-bar blues*, a blues progression consisting of twelve repeated bars of music.

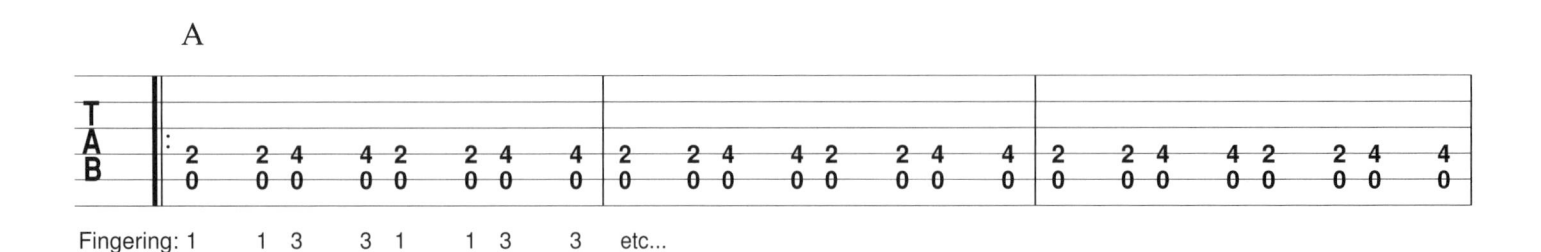

Fingering: 1   1 3   3 1   1 3   3   etc...

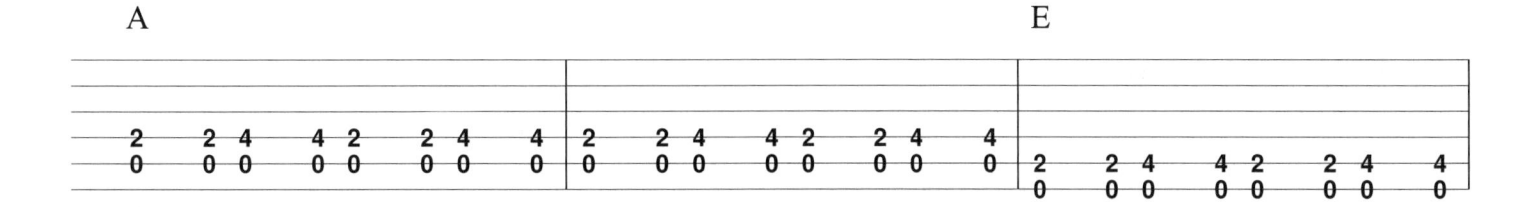

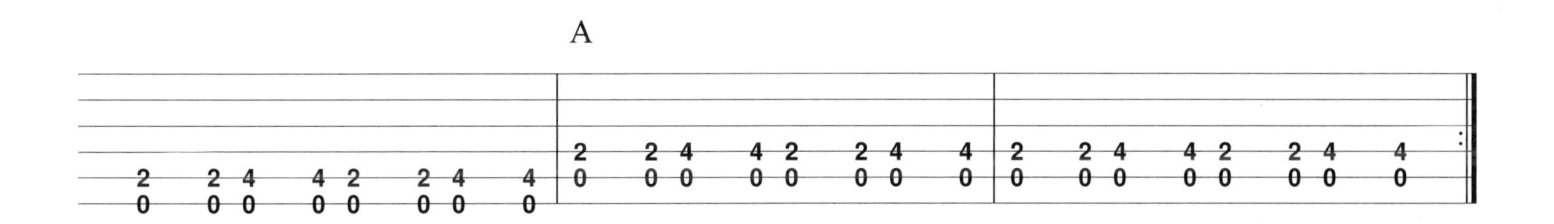

```
    A                                                    E
|------------------------------------|------------------------------------|------------------------------------|
|------------------------------------|------------------------------------|------------------------------------|
|--2---2-4---4-2---2-4---4--|-2---2-4---4-2---2-4---4--|------------------------------------|
|--0---0-0---0-0---0-0---0--|-0---0-0---0-0---0-0---0--|--2---2-4---4-2---2-4---4--|
|                                               |                                               |--0---0-0---0-0---0-0---0--|
|------------------------------------|------------------------------------|------------------------------------|
```

```
                                A
|------------------------------------|------------------------------------|------------------------------------||
|------------------------------------|------------------------------------|------------------------------------||
|------------------------------------|--2---2-4---4-2---2-4---4--|-2---2-4---4-2---2-4---4--||
|--2---2-4---4-2---2-4---4--|--0---0-0---0-0---0-0---0--|-0---0-0---0-0---0-0---0--||
|--0---0-0---0-0---0-0---0--|                                               |                                               ||
|------------------------------------|------------------------------------|------------------------------------||
```

Blues is played with a *shuffle feel*, also called a triplet feel. This example was written in eighth notes and the second eighth note of each beat should lag a little. This is referred to as triplet feel because the beat is actually divided by thirds, counted as if there were three eighth notes per beat instead of two. The first part of the beat gets 2/3 of a beat, and the second part only gets 1/3.

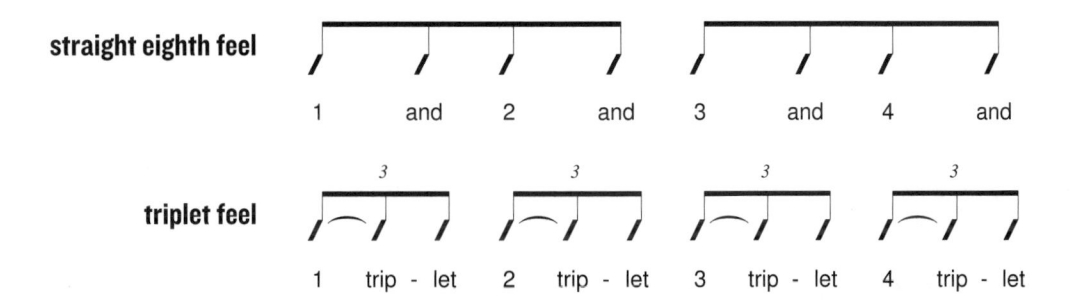

straight eighth feel

1   and   2   and   3   and   4   and

triplet feel

1   trip - let   2   trip - let   3   trip - let   4   trip - let

Shuffle feel is a much easier concept to understand by hearing it. Listen to the backing track, count along and try to get the triplet feel in your head. Also, check out almost any blues standard, slow or fast, and you'll probably recognize a shuffle feel being used.

CHAPTER 2

The Minor Pentatonic Scale

Minor pentatonic scales are the most commonly used scales for playing rock and blues solos. The pentatonic is a five note scale, or an abbreviated version of the full natural minor scale. The word "pentatonic" comes from the greek words, "penta" (five) and "tonic" (the keynote).

Memorize and practice this scale; it's the one you'll use most often for playing melodies and leads. There are five different positions of this scale, each beginning on a different note of the scale. All five positions are shown here in tab. To the right of each tab staff is a scale diagram. These are similar to the chord diagrams we've previously used. A scale diagram shows you all the notes in the scale within a certain position on the neck. The stacked numbers below the diagram indicate the fingering for the notes on each string.

1st Position A Minor Pentatonic Scale

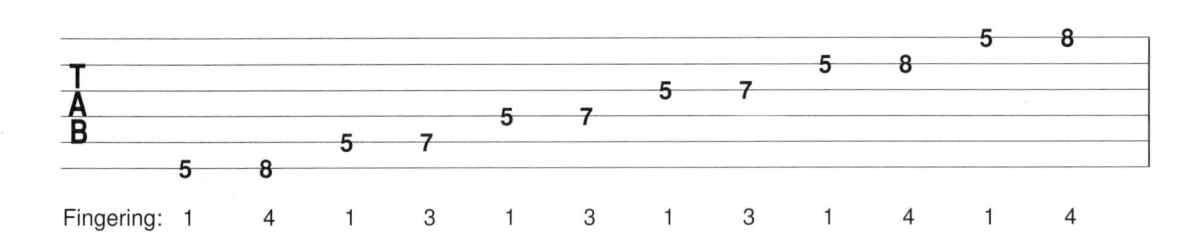

Fingering: 1 4 1 3 1 3 1 3 1 4 1 4

1st position, 5fr

1 1 1 1 1 1
4 3 3 3 4 4

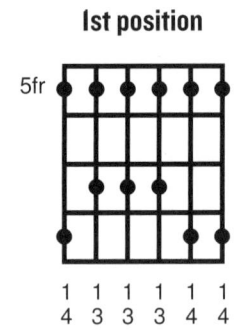

2nd Position A Minor Pentatonic Scale

Fingering: 2 4 1 4 1 4 1 3 2 4 2 4

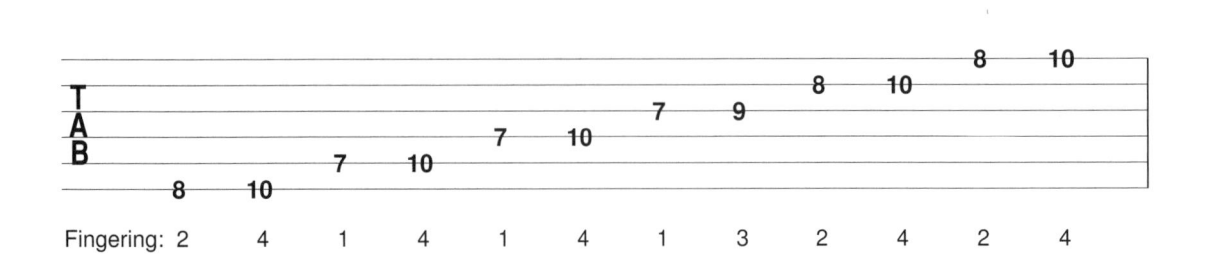

2nd position, 8fr

2 1 1 1 2 2
4 4 4 3 4 4

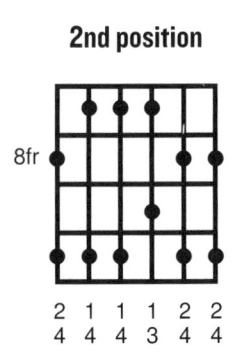

3rd Position A Minor Pentatonic Scale

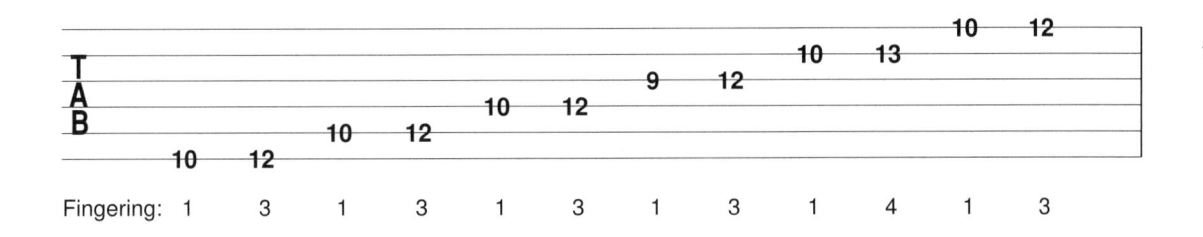

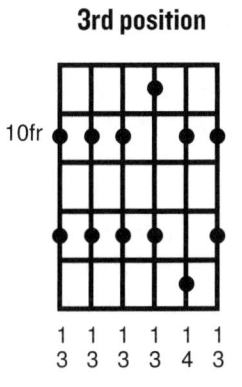

```
T ---------------------------------------10--12--
A -------------------------------10--13-----------
B --------------------9---12----------------------
  -----------10--12-------------------------------
  --10--12----------------------------------------
```

Fingering: 1   3   1   3   1   3   1   3   1   4   1   3

3rd position

10fr

1 1 1 1 1 1
3 3 3 3 4 3

4th Position A Minor Pentatonic Scale

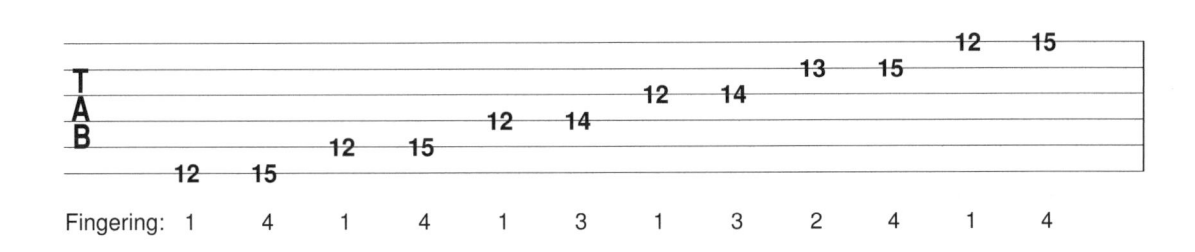

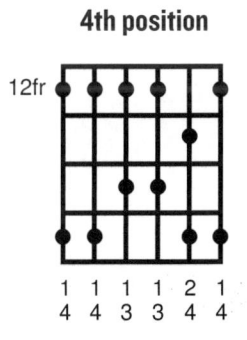

```
T ---------------------------------------12--15--
A -------------------------------13--15-----------
B --------------------12--14----------------------
  -----------12--14-------------------------------
  --12--15----------------------------------------
```

Fingering: 1   4   1   4   1   3   1   3   2   4   1   4

4th position

12fr

1 1 1 1 2 1
4 4 3 3 4 4

5th Position A Minor Pentatonic Scale

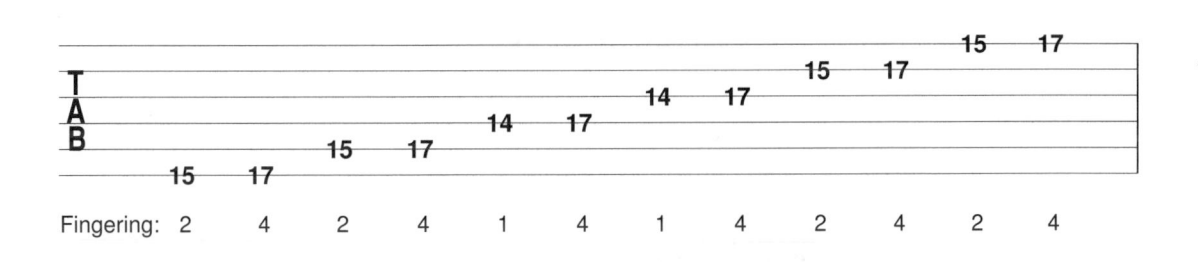

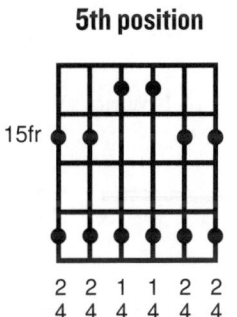

```
T ---------------------------------------15--17--
A -------------------------------15--17-----------
B --------------------14--17----------------------
  -----------14--17-------------------------------
  --15--17----------------------------------------
```

Fingering: 2   4   2   4   1   4   1   4   2   4   2   4

5th position

15fr

2 2 1 1 2 2
4 4 4 4 4 4

23

Minor Pentatonic Scale Fretboard Diagram

Once you have all five positions of the minor pentatonic scales mastered, you'll be able to play solos in any position on the neck. Remember that there are only five different name notes in the scale, and the different positions are just groupings of these same notes in different octaves and different places on the neck. The 4th and 5th positions from the previous page can be transposed one octave lower (shown below in the fretboard diagram). Notice how each position overlaps the next; the left side of one position is the right side of the next one and so on. Think of these scale positions as building blocks (like Legos). When soloing, you can move from position to position and play across the entire fretboard.

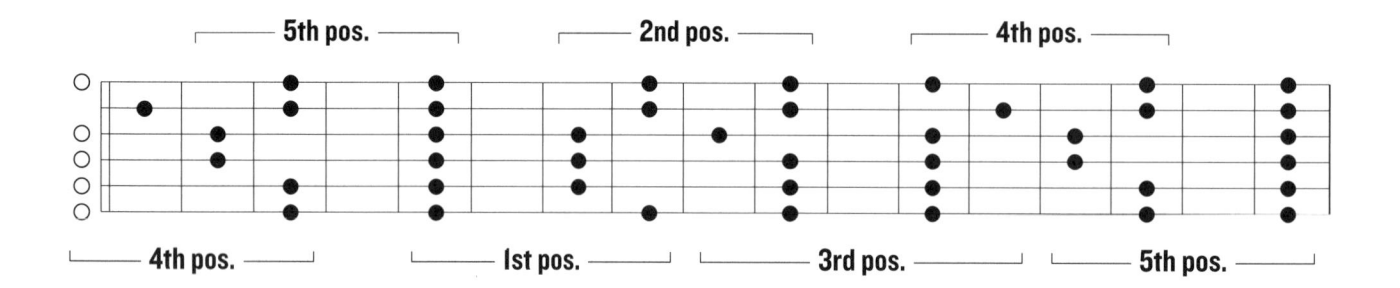

Alternate Picking

Consistent use of alternate picking is a very good habit for you to have. Alternate picking allows you to play solos with much more control and accuracy. Practice playing all of the minor pentatonic scale positions using alternate picking. Play each position ascending and descending at a steady, even tempo until the picking motion feels natural.

The following symbols are used to show picking (or strumming) directions:

⊓ - downpick (pick down toward the floor)

V - uppick (pick up toward the ceiling)

Lead Patterns

The following examples are standard lead pattern exercises, designed to help you build coordination and learn how to begin using the minor pentatonics for playing leads. Use alternate picking and the metronome to start out slowly and get the rhythm. Memorize the patterns and gradually speed up the tempo. Before you know it, you'll be playing blazing rock and blues guitar solos.

Double Lead Pattern

19-20 DISC 1

Here is the 1st position A minor pentatonic scale played using a doubling pattern. Play the notes on the 5th through 2nd strings twice as you travel up and down the scale. Use alternate picking and a steady, even tempo.

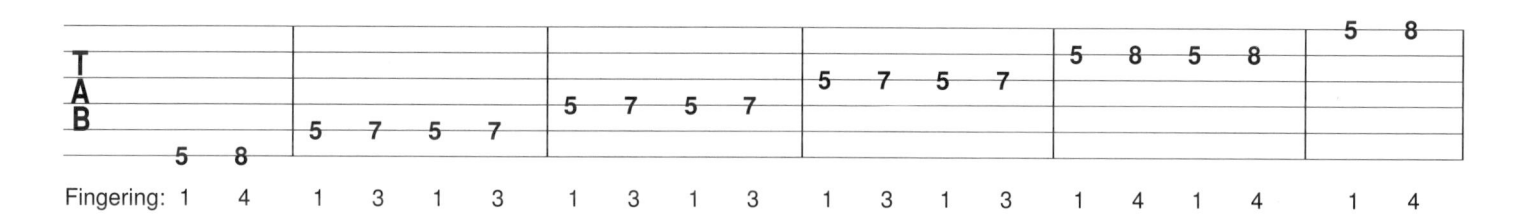

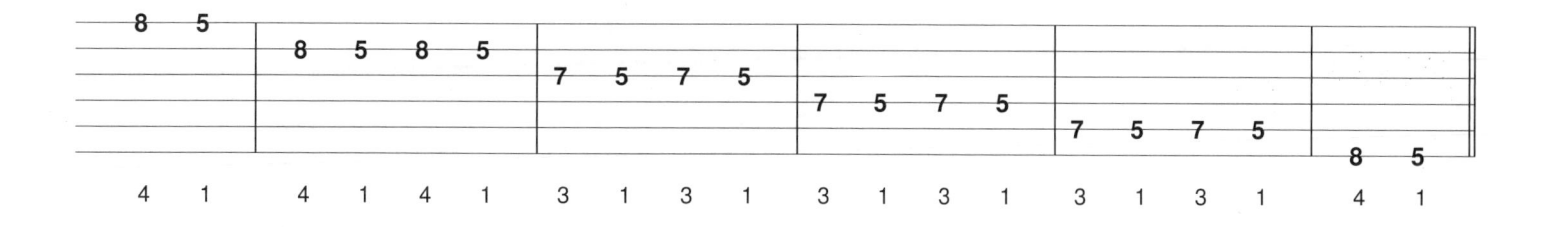

```
T|-----------------|-----------------|-----------------|-----------------|----5--8--5--8---|---5--8---|
A|-----------------|-----------------|-----5--7--5--7--|--5--7--5--7-----|-----------------|----------|
B|-----5--8--------|--5--7--5--7-----|-----------------|-----------------|-----------------|----------|
```
Fingering: 1 4   1 3 1 3   1 3 1 3   1 3 1 3   1 4 1 4   1 4

```
|--8--5-----------|--8--5--8--5-----|-----------------|-----------------|-----------------|----------|
|-----------------|-----------------|--7--5--7--5-----|--7--5--7--5-----|--7--5--7--5-----|----------|
|-----------------|-----------------|-----------------|-----------------|-----------------|--8--5----|
```
  4 1   4 1 4 1   3 1 3 1   3 1 3 1   3 1 3 1   4 1

Now let's take the same double lead pattern and transpose it to the 2nd positon. Once you've got these two memorized, transpose the pattern to the other positions of the pentatonic scale.

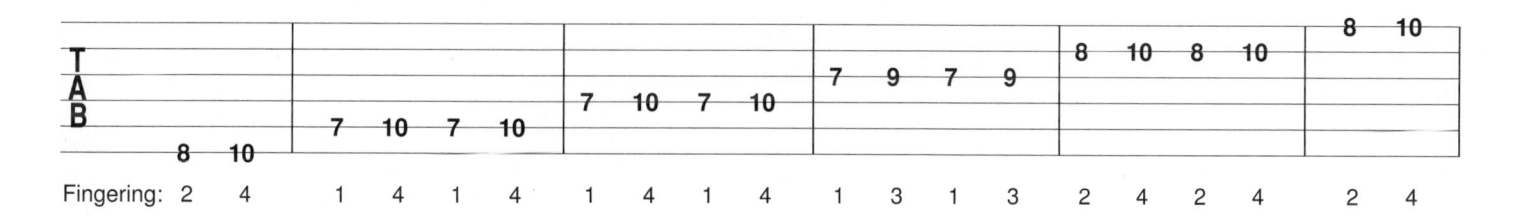

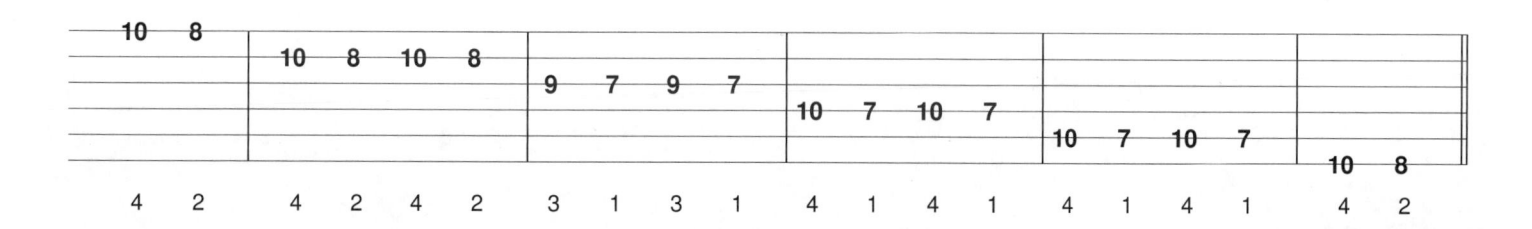

```
T|-----------------|-----------------|-----------------|-------------------|---8--10--8--10--|--8--10--|
A|-----------------|-----------------|-----7--10--7--10|--7--9--7--9-------|-----------------|---------|
B|-----8--10-------|--7--10--7--10---|-----------------|-------------------|-----------------|---------|
```
Fingering: 2 4   1 4 1 4   1 4 1 4   1 3 1 3   2 4 2 4   2 4

```
|--10--8----------|--10--8--10--8---|-----------------|-----------------|-----------------|----------|
|-----------------|-----------------|--9--7--9--7-----|--10--7--10--7---|--10--7--10--7---|----------|
|-----------------|-----------------|-----------------|-----------------|-----------------|--10--8---|
```
  4 2   4 2 4 2   3 1 3 1   4 1 4 1   4 1 4 1   4 2

Triplet Lead Pattern

Here is the 1st position A minor pentatonic scale played in groups of three notes, or triplets. Count "one - two - three, one - two - three" out loud while you play through this exercise to get the triplet feel in your head.

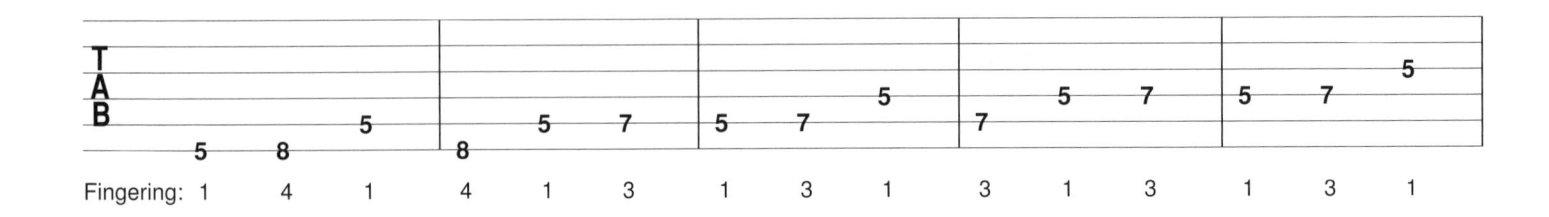

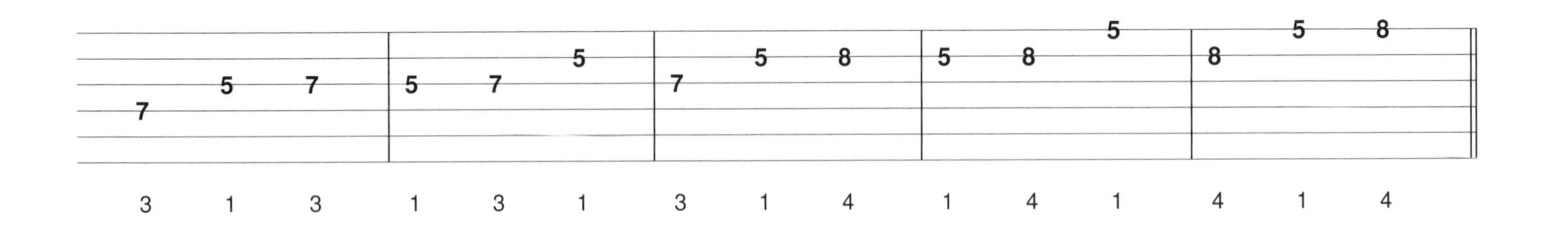

```
T|-------------------------------------------------------------------5-|
A|-----------------5-----5--7--5--7-----5-----5--7--5--7-------------|
B|--5--8-----8-----------------------7-----7-------------------------|
     5   8   5   8
```
Fingering: 1 4 1 4 1 3 1 3 1 3 1 3 1 3 1

```
|----------------------------5-----5--8--5--8-----5-----5--8-|
|----5--7--5--7-----5--8--5--8-----------------8-----8-------|
|-7-----------7------------------------------------------------|
```
 3 1 3 1 3 1 3 1 4 1 4 1 4 1 4

Now let's play the same pattern in reverse, back down the scale in triplets.

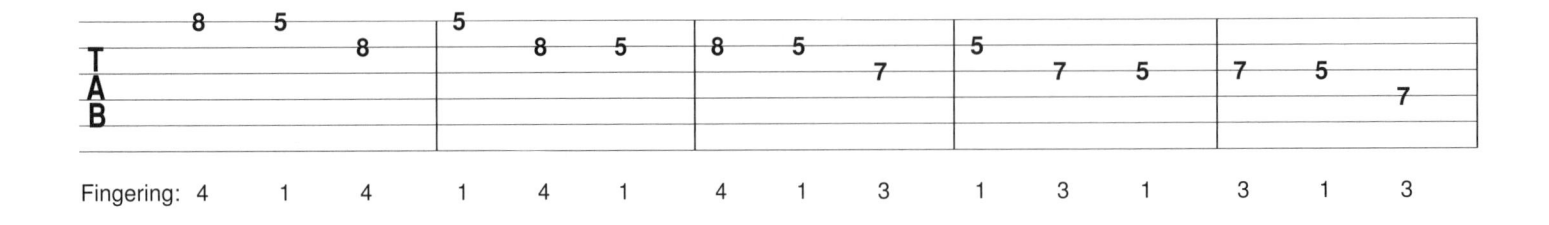

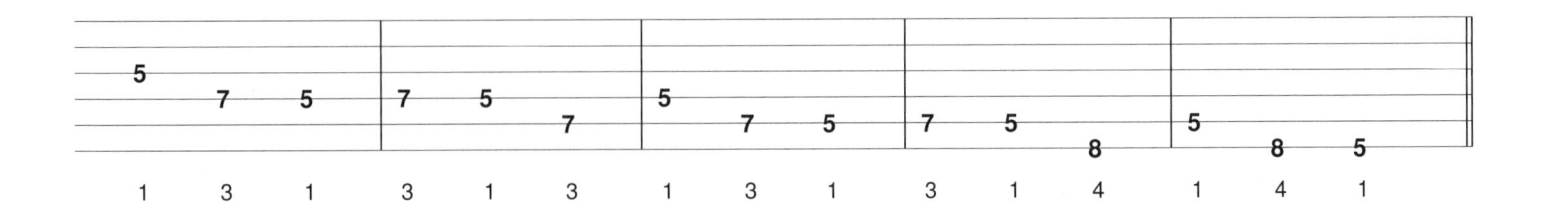

```
|--8--5-----5-----------------------------------------------|
|--------8-----8--5--8--5--8--5-----5-----5-----5-----------|
|---------------------------7-----7--5--7--5-------7--------|
```
Fingering: 4 1 4 1 4 1 4 1 3 1 3 1 3 1 3

```
|-----5-------------------------------------------------------|
|--------7--5--7--5-----5-----7--5--7--5-----5--------------|
|-----------------7-----7-----------------8-----8--5--------|
```
 1 3 1 3 1 3 1 3 1 3 1 4 1 4 1

26

Practice every position of the A minor pentatonic scale using the tripet lead pattern and alternate picking. The 2nd position ascending and descending triplet patterns are shown below.

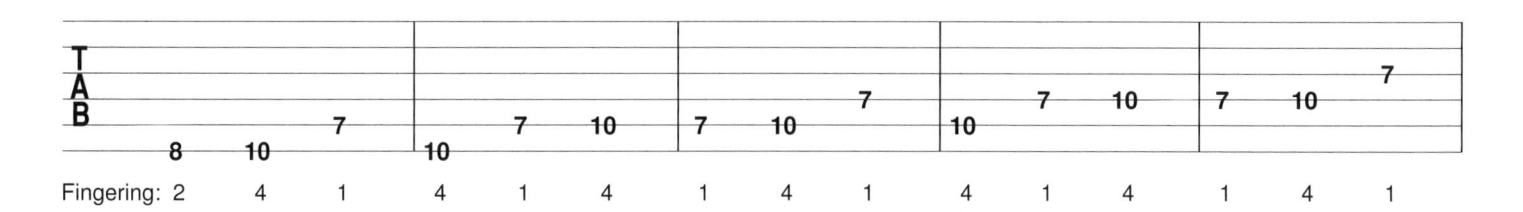

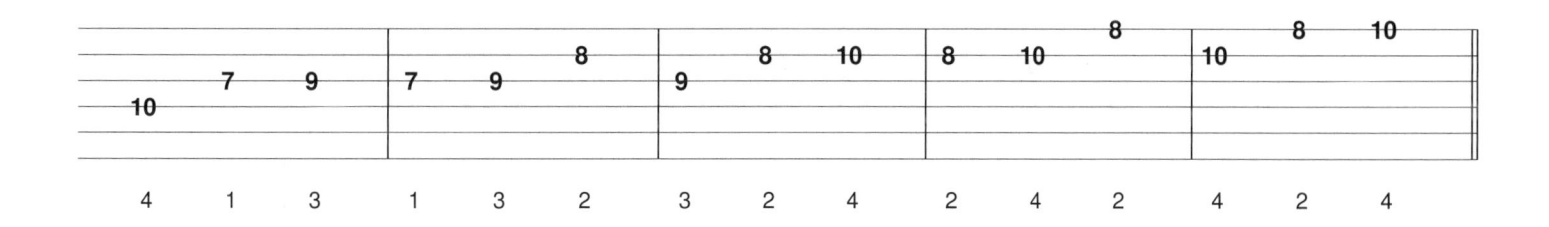

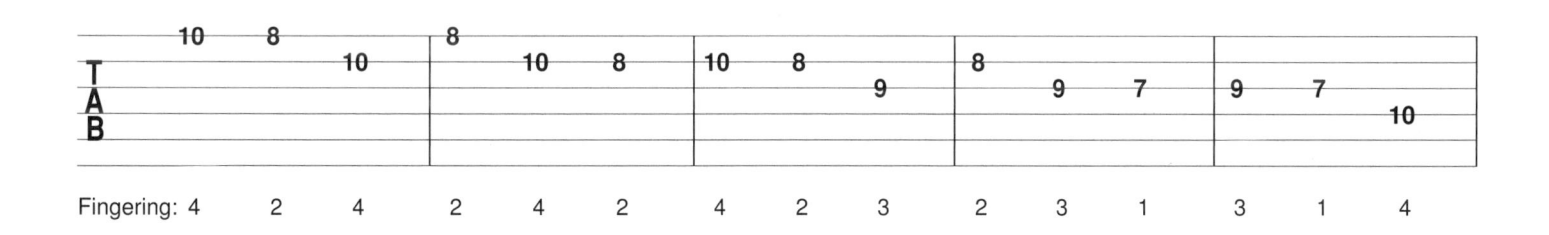

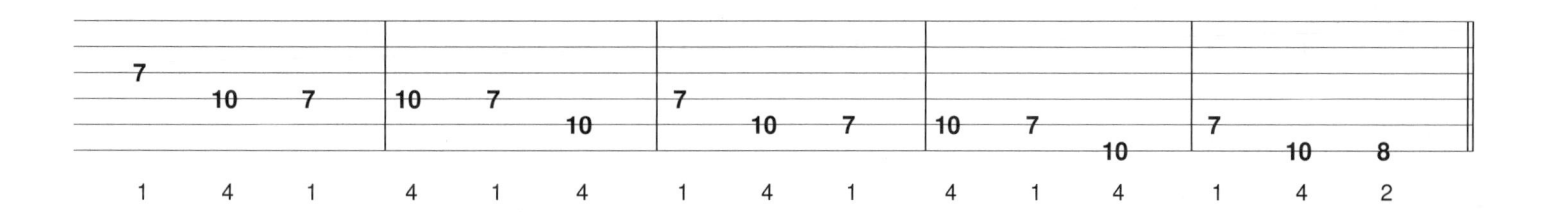

```
T|-----------------------------------------------------------------------------7-|
A|-------------------------------------------------7----7---10---7---10----------|
B|----------7-------7---10---7---10---10---7---10--------------------------------|
  -8---10-------10-------------------------------------------------------------
Fingering: 2   4   1   4   1   4   1   4   1   4   1   4   1   4   1
```

```
|----------------------------------------------------------8--------8---10--||
|---------------------------8--------8---10---8---10---10-------10----------||
|----7----9----7----9----9----------------------------------------------------||
|-10--------------------------------------------------------------------------||
  4    1    3    1    3    2    3    2    4    2    4    2    4    2    4
```

```
    -10---8-----8------------------------------------------------------------
T|-------10-----10---8---10---8----8----------------------------------------
A|-----------------------------9-------9---7----9---7----------------------
B|----------------------------------------------------10-------------------
Fingering: 4   2   4   2   4   2   4   2   3   2   3   1   3   1   4
```

```
 -7-----------------------------------------------------------------------
 ----10---7---10---7----7------------------------------------------------
 ------------------10-------10---7---10---7----7---------------------10--8
 -----------------------------------------------10----10---8------------||
   1    4   1    4   1    4   1    4    1   4    1   4    1    4   2
```

Quick Tip!

PLAY SLOWLY AT FIRST

When learning something new, don't start out trying to play it as fast as possible. Take things slowly at first; play slow enough so you don't keep making mistakes. Build your speed over time. A great tool for learning to build speed gradually is a metronome. This is a device that clicks at an adjustable rate that you set. A metronome allows you to gauge your progress each day. By playing along with the click, you learn to play in time with other instruments.

Lead Techniques

Bending

Now let's learn some lead guitar techniques that will add expression to your playing. Bends are a very soulful way of creating emotion with the guitar, using flesh against steel to alter and control pitches. All guitarists have their own unique, signature way of bending notes.

The row of tab staffs below show bends using the third, fourth or first fingers. The "B" above the staff indicates a bend, and the arrow with a "1" above it means to bend the note one whole step in pitch.

First try the third finger bend. While fretting the note with your third finger, keep your first two fingers down on the string behind it and push upward using all three fingers. This will give you added coordination and control. Use the same technique for the fourth finger bend, using all four fingers to bend the string upward. The first finger bend will probably be the hardest since you are only using one finger to bend the string. In some situations, you may even pull the string downward with your first finger to bend the note.

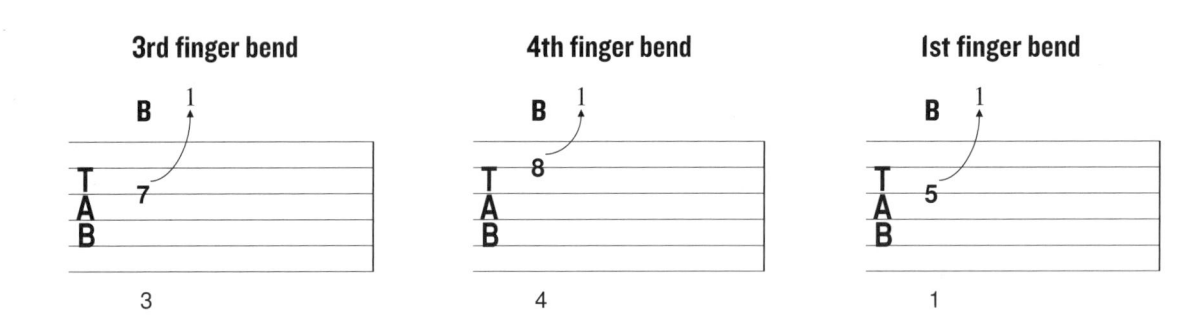

3rd finger bend   **4th finger bend**   **1st finger bend**

The following example shows what the bends might look like in context when playing a solo in the 1st position A minor pentatonic scale. Play through this exercise and start to get a feel for how to incorporate bends into your own riffs.

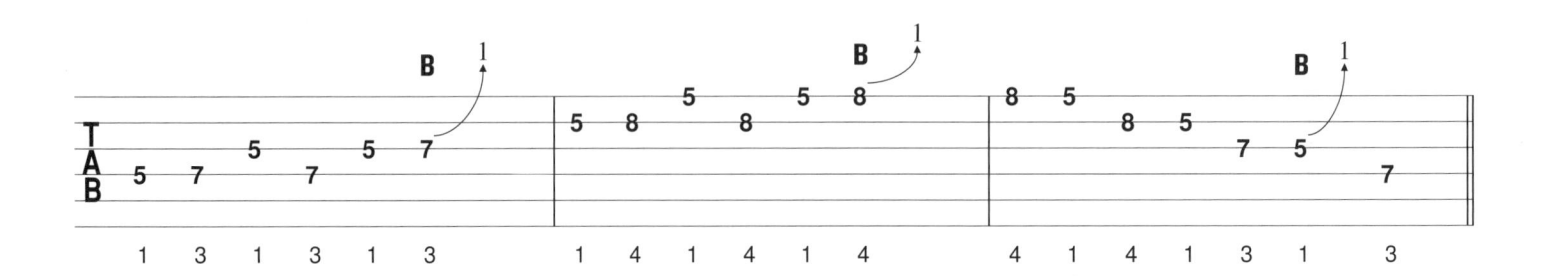

Hammer Ons

A hammer on is also a widely used lead technique. On the staff below, you'll see a slur connecting one tab number to the next. This indicates that only the first tab number is picked; the second note is not struck. The "H" above the slur indicates a hammer on.

To play a hammer on, pick the first note and then push down the next note using just your left hand finger (without picking it). Play through the following series of hammer ons to see how you can use them with the minor pentatonic scale.

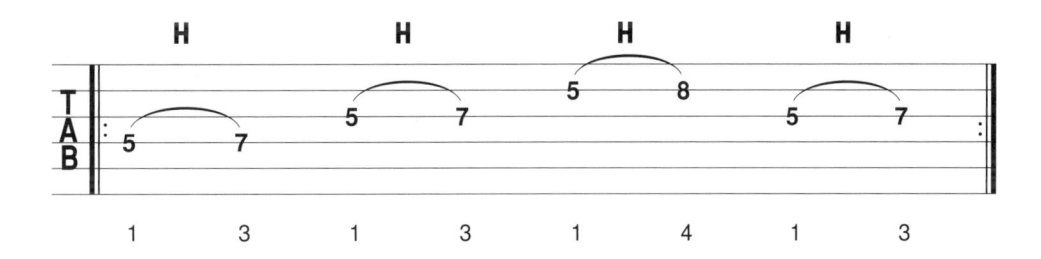

```
   H        H        H         H
               5    8
        5    7             5    7
T||:5    7
A
B
   1    3   1    3   1    4   1    3
```

Pull Offs

Pull offs are the opposite of hammer ons. Pick the first note and pull or snap your finger off the string to the get the second note. Your first finger should already be in place, fretting the second note in advance. The "P" above each slur below indicates a pull off.

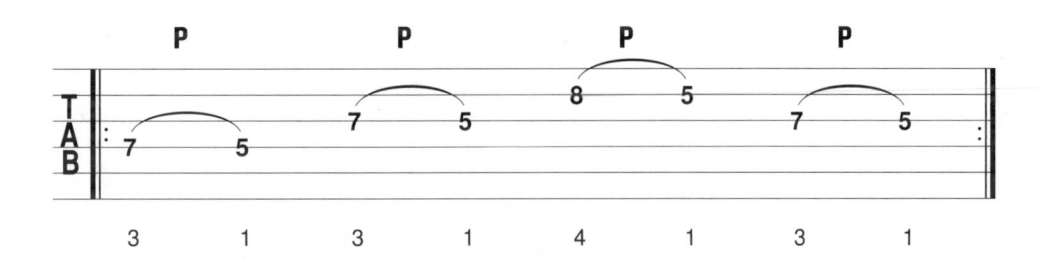

```
   P        P        P         P
                8    5
        7    5             7    5
T||:7    5
A
B
   3    1   3    1   4    1   3    1
```

Complete Blues Lead

Here's a solo that uses all of the previous lead techniques in various positions on the neck. In the 11th measure, there's an example of a bend and release: after bending the note, gradually release the bend to the note's original pitch.

Refer to the CD or download the backing track from www.rockhousemethod.com and practice playing along with the band. This is a I - IV - V progression in A that also uses a shuffle feel. The chord names above the tab staff are there for a reference to show you where the changes are.

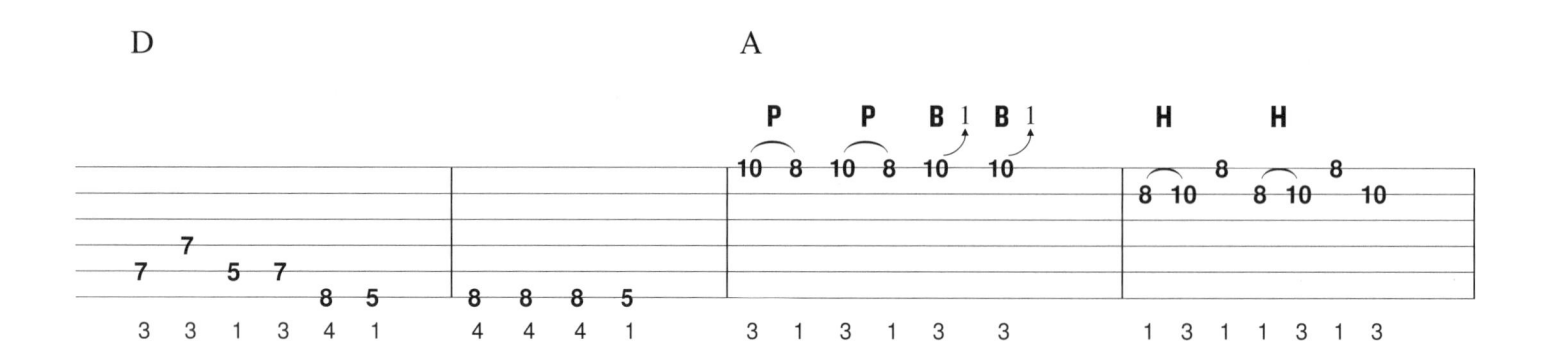

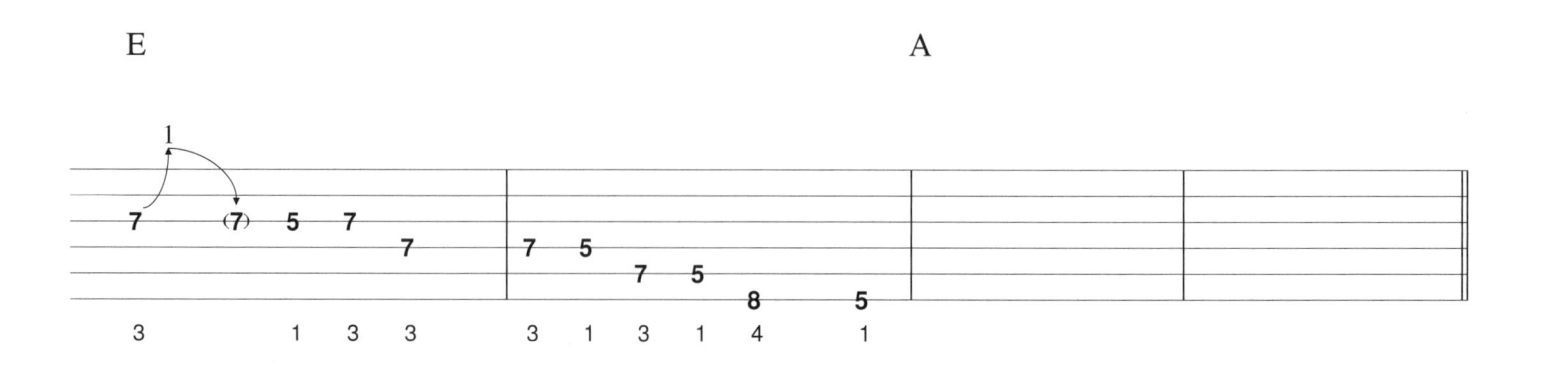

CHAPTER 3

Creating a Great Blues Sound

Effect pedals (or *stomp boxes*) are often used to enhance or distort a guitar's tone. There are many different types of effects. The most popular effects used for blues guitar are overdrive, distortion, chorus, delay, reverb, and wah wah. Below are a few of the most common ones. Take a trip to your local music store and try out a variety of effect pedals to hear which ones sound good to you.

Overdrive Pedal

A distortion or overdrive pedal simulates the sound of the guitar's signal being overdriven, giving it a fuzz tone. Overdrive can be used in different degrees. Light distortion will give the sound a warm, round, or full tone. Using heavy distortion gives the guitar a heavy metal tone.

Chorus Pedal

A chorus pedal creates the sound of a few guitars played at once. A chorus doubles the original signal with a very slight delay, causing a wavy tone that simulates a chorus of guitars.

Wah Wah Pedal

A wah wah pedal is a foot activated pedal that you can "play" with your foot while playing the guitar. The pedal gets rocked back and forth by your foot and gives the guitar a talking, wah wah type sound. What a wah wah pedal actually does is sweep quickly back and forth between extreme bass and extreme treble driven by the movement of your foot.

Amplifier Gain

Turning up the gain knob on an amplifier overdrives the signal and creates distortion. Use small amounts of gain for a warm, thick tone. Using high gain will cause heavy distortion. Use the gain in conjunction with the amplifier's master volume control to set the desired tone and level of the sound.

Blues Riffs That Will Make Yo Mama Scream

Here's a collection of little riffs that will help you start building your own bag of tricks. These riffs use various positons of the A minor pentatonic scales, and incorporate all of the techniques we've covered so far. You can play all of these riffs at different speeds, with or without a shuffle feel, starting on any beat you choose. Any one of these is a good choice when soloing and improvising. Try coming up with some of your own variations.

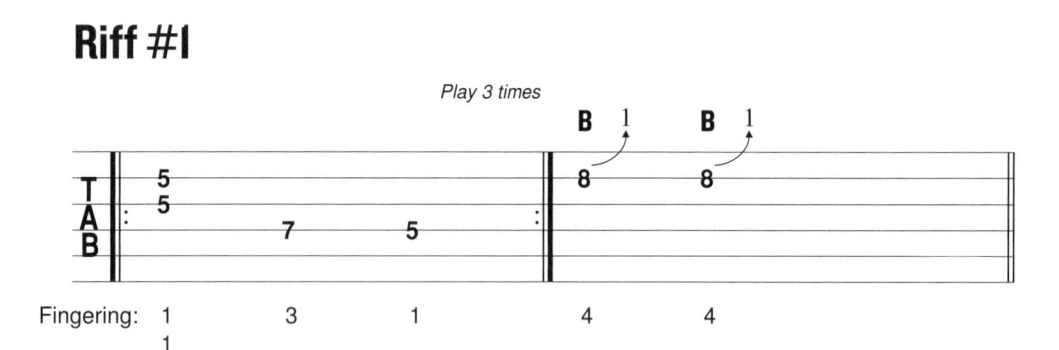

Riff #1

Play 3 times

```
T|--5----------------------||--8--------8--------|
A|--5----7----5------------||--------------------|
B|-------------------------||--------------------|
```

Fingering: 1   3   1   4   4
            1

Riff #2

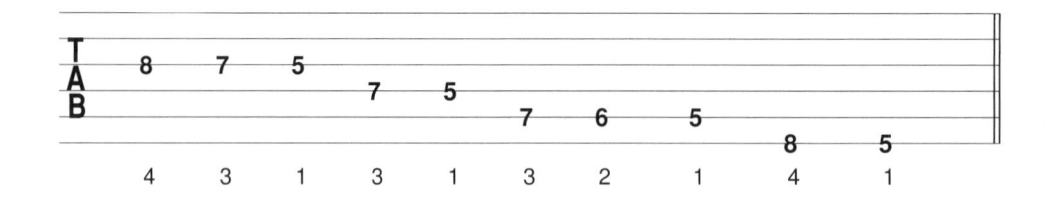

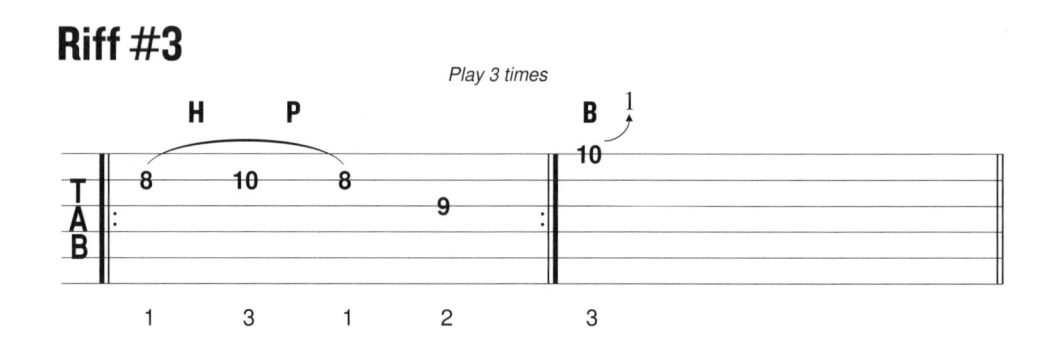

```
T|--8--7--5------------------------|
A|--------7--5---------------------|
B|-------------7--6--5--------8--5-|
```
           4   3   1   3   1   3   2   1   4   1

Riff #3

Play 3 times

H   P   B
```
T|--8--10--8---------||--10----------------|
A|-----------9-------||--------------------|
B|-------------------||--------------------|
```
   1   3   1   2   3

Riff #4

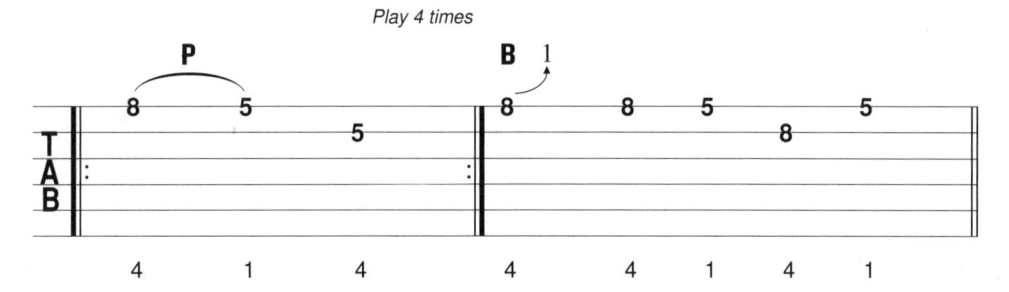

Play 4 times

Riff #5

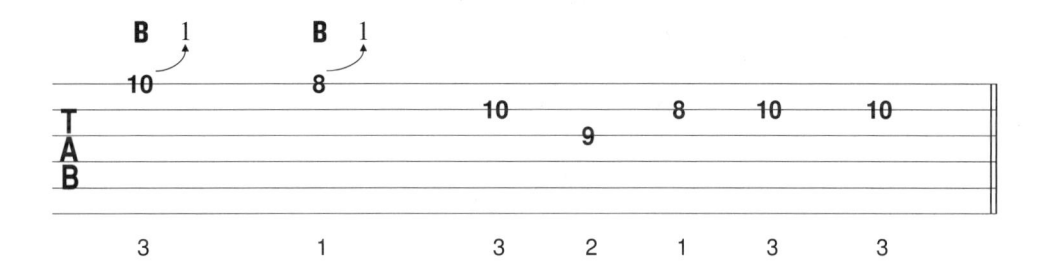

Quick Tip!

DEVELOP GOOD PRACTICE HABITS

Knowing how to practice efficiently will accelerate your progress. Set aside a certain amount of time for practicing and have a routine that reviews all of the techniques you know. Create your own exercises that target weaknesses in your playing. It's important to experiment and get creative as well; try things fast or slow, light or hard, soft or loud.

The B. B. Box

The B.B. box is a section of the minor pentatonic scale that overlaps the 1st and 2nd positions. The name refers to the great B.B. King because he bases a lot of his soloing around this scale. The following fretboard diagram indicates which notes are in the B.B. Box (in the key of Am) using solid black dots. The open circles show the minor pentatonic scale notes in the surrounding positions. Refer to the tab staff below the diagram for the proper fingering.

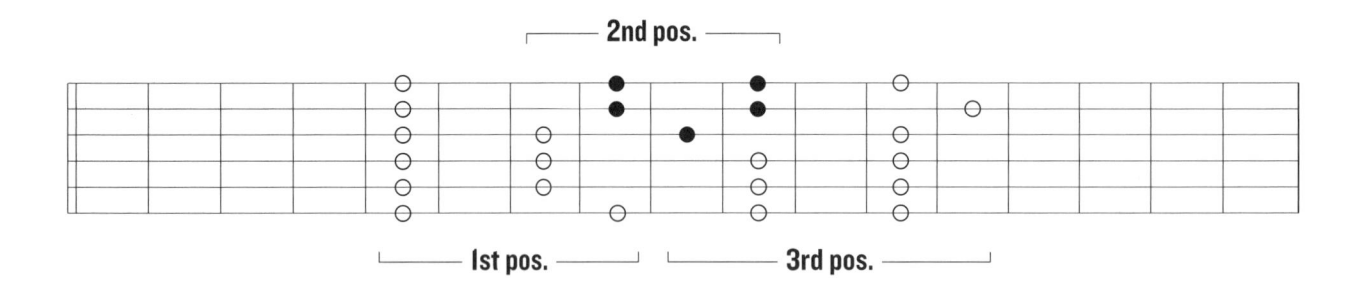

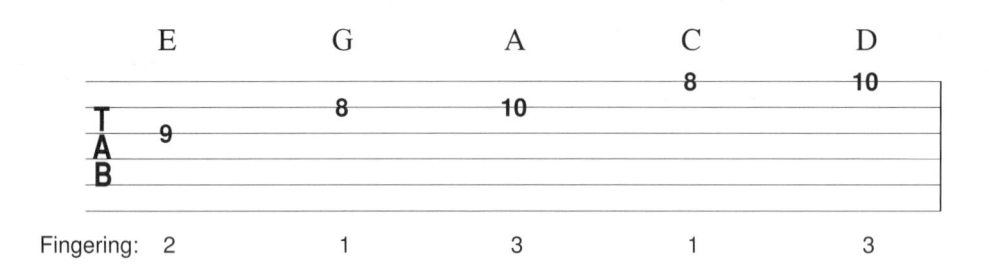

```
         E        G        A        C        D
                                    8       10
                  8       10
T        9
A
B
```

Fingering: 2   1   3   1   3

Above each tab number is its note name. Notice that A (the *root note*) is in between the other notes of the scale. The B.B. Box takes the five notes of the minor pentatonic scale and puts the root note in the middle. This position allows you to play around the root note, playing a few notes up or a few notes down from it. This is also the way many blues singers arrange their vocal melodies. The B.B. Box is great for soloing off the vocal melody or for trading riffs back and forth with the singer.

Shuffle Blues Rhythm

This progression incorporates chords and single notes to make up the rhythm. This standard blues rhythm is in A and uses a I - IV - V progression. Practice along with the backing track to get the timing and the shuffle feel.

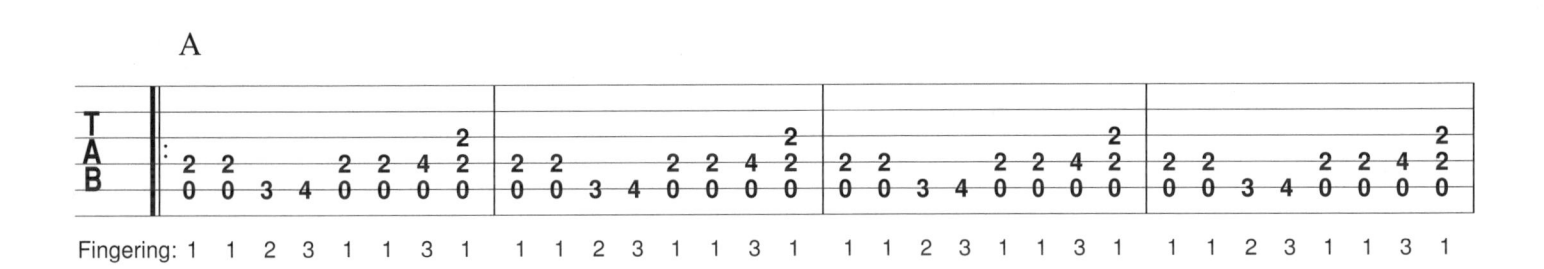

A

```
                2                       2                       2                       2
  2 2       2 2 4 2    2 2       2 2 4 2    2 2       2 2 4 2    2 2       2 2 4 2
  0 0 3 4 0 0 0 0      0 0 3 4 0 0 0 0      0 0 3 4 0 0 0 0      0 0 3 4 0 0 0 0
```
Fingering: 1 1 2 3 1 1 3 1   1 1 2 3 1 1 3 1   1 1 2 3 1 1 3 1   1 1 2 3 1 1 3 1

D   A

```
              3                       3                                 2                       2
2 2       2 2 4 2    2 2       2 2 4 2    2 2       2 2 4 2    2 2       2 2 4 2
0 0 3 4 0 0 0        0 0 3 4 0 0 0        0 0 3 4 0 0 0 0      0 0 3 4 0 0 0 0
```
1 1 2 3 1 1 3 2   1 1 2 3 1 1 3 2   1 1 2 3 1 1 3 1   1 1 2 3 1 1 3 1
                        1   1

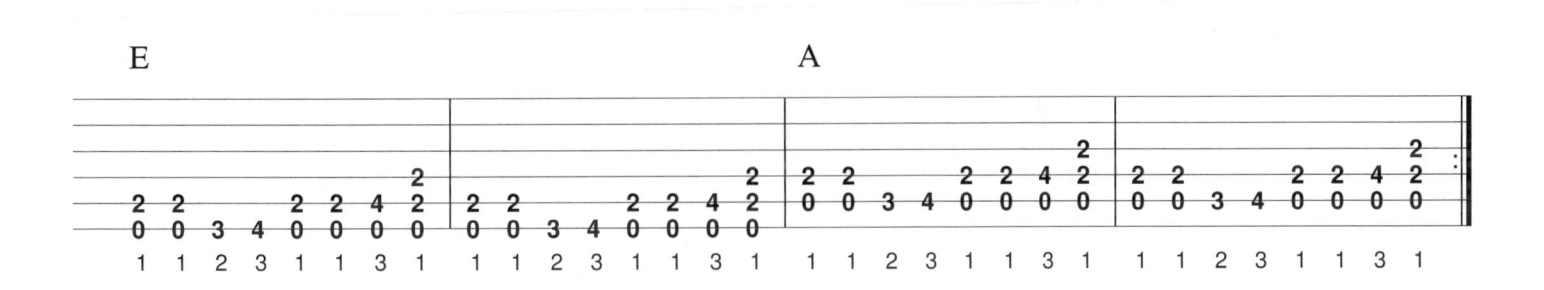

E   A

```
                                                  2                       2
              2                       2    2 2       2 2 4 2    2 2       2 2 4 2
2 2       2 2 4 2    2 2       2 2 4 2    0 0 3 4 0 0 0 0      0 0 3 4 0 0 0 0
0 0 3 4 0 0 0 0      0 0 3 4 0 0 0 0
```
1 1 2 3 1 1 3 1   1 1 2 3 1 1 3 1   1 1 2 3 1 1 3 1   1 1 2 3 1 1 3 1

Full Blues Lead

Here's an example of a solo that can be played over the shuffle blues rhythm you've just learned. This solo incorporates bends, hammer ons and pull offs in a variety of positions. The riff in the first measure is one of the most commonly used blues riffs; it can be heard in countless blues guitar solos. After you've got this solo down, try to create your own using the different lead techniques and all five positions of the A minor pentatonic scales.

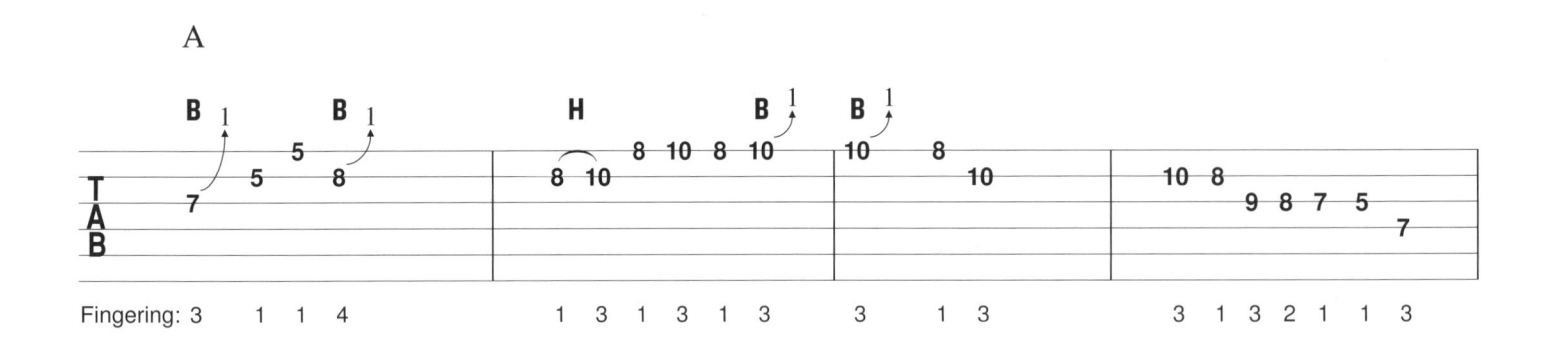

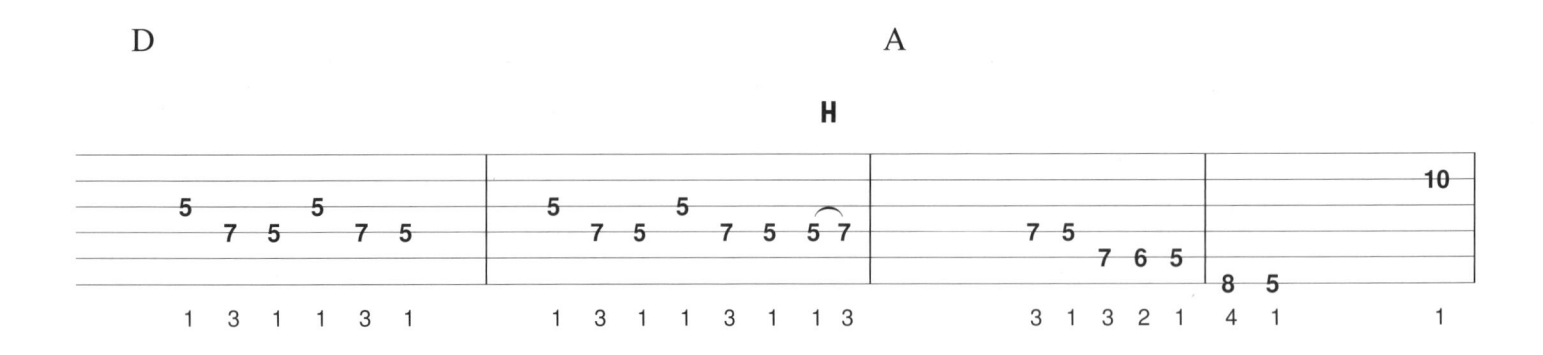

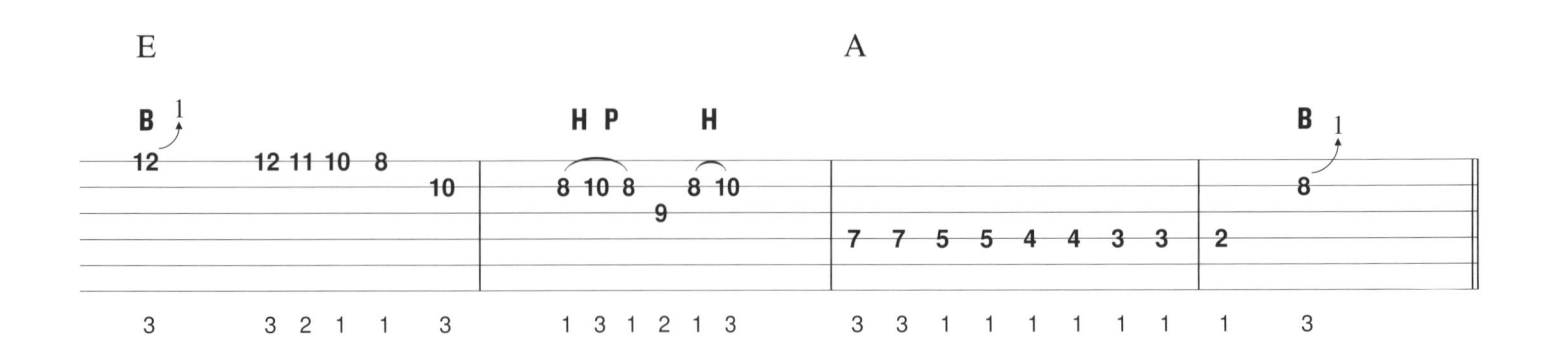

House of Blues is the Home of Live Entertainment.

Have an intimate yet high energy experience at one of our many venues across the country.

CHAPTER 4

Barre Chords

Let's begin this section by expanding your chord vocabulary. The following full barre chords contain no open strings, so they are *moveable* chords; you can transpose them to any fret. After mastering these chords, you'll be able to play in any key and position on the guitar.

6th String Barre Chords

The first chord is F major. This chord is especially difficult to play because you need to barre across all six strings with your first finger, then add the other three notes as well. Pick out each note individually to make sure the chord sounds clean.

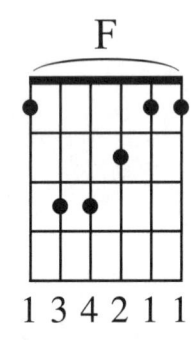

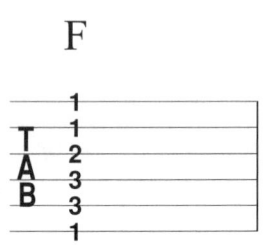

Notice that the lowest note of the chord is F, the *root note*. Using the musical alphabet, you can move barre chords up the neck and change them to any chord in the scale. Use the following chart to find any chord along the 6th string by moving the F chord. The name of the chord will change depending on which fret you move the chord to.

6th string notes (F chord)	E	F	F#	G	G#	A	A#	B	C	C#	D	D#	E
fret number	Open	1	2	3	4	5	6	7	8	9	10	11	12

Once you've learned the F barre chord, simply lift your second finger and you'll have the Fm barre chord. The F7 (also called the *F dominant seventh*) barre chord is only slightly different from the F as well; just reposition your fourth finger and you've got it. Dominant seventh chords are often used in blues as substitutes for major chords.

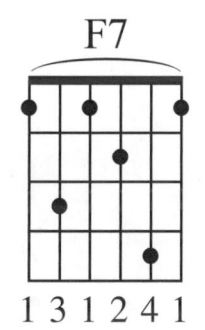

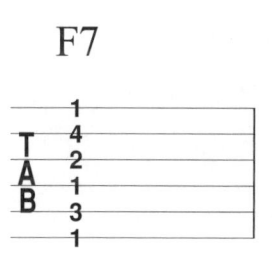

Fm

1 3 4 1 1 1

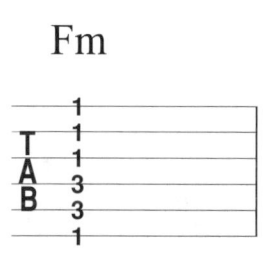

F7

1 3 1 2 4 1

5th String Barre Chords

The B♭ major barre chord is played at the 1st fret with the root note on the 5th string. This chord has a third finger barre. Make sure the 1st and 6th strings are muted and not strummed. Use the chart below to transpose this chord to any other fret along the 5th string.

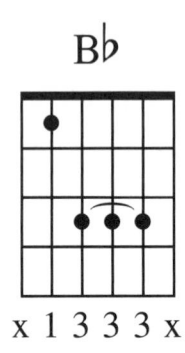

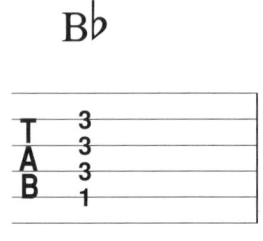

B♭

x 1 3 3 3 x

B♭

```
T  3
A  3
B  3
   1
```

5th string notes (B♭ chord)	A	B♭	B	C	C♯	D	D♯	E	F	F♯	G	G♯	A
fret number	Open	1	2	3	4	5	6	7	8	9	10	11	12

Quick Tip!

ALWAYS TUNE YOUR GUITAR

Make sure your guitar is in tune every time you play it. You could be playing all of the right notes, but they'll sound incorrect if you haven't tuned up. Even if only one string is slightly out of tune, the simplest of chords will sound bad. It's a good idea to stop and check your tuning from time to time while practicing.

The B♭m and B♭7 barre chords are played using a first finger barre. Once you have them mastered, try transposing both chords to other frets using the 5th string chart on the previous page.

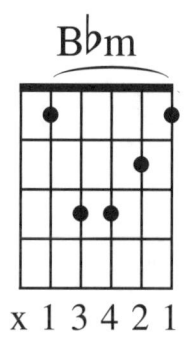

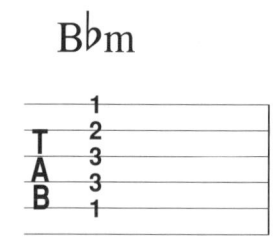

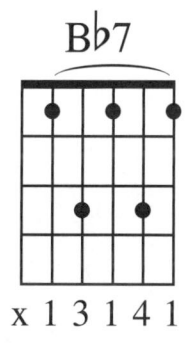

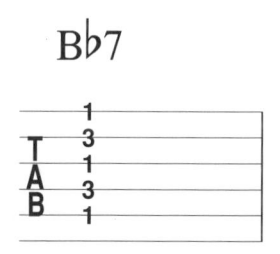

Understanding the 12 Bar Blues Concept

12-bar blues is a progression based on the I - IV - V chords that is 12 measures long. Most blues music is made up of 12-bar blues progressions; 12 measures of music that repeat throughout the song. This particular example combines barre chords and single notes in the key of A. The single notes at the end of each measure are played with the first and third fingers in the same positon as each chord. Play along with the backing track to get the shuffle feel.

A

```
T|--5-5-5-5-5-5--------|--5-5-5-5-5-5--------|--5-5-5-5-5-5--------|--5-5-5-5-5-5--------|
A|--5-5-5-5-5-5--------|--5-5-5-5-5-5--------|--5-5-5-5-5-5--------|--5-5-5-5-5-5--------|
B|--6-6-6-6-6-6--------|--6-6-6-6-6-6--------|--6-6-6-6-6-6--------|--6-6-6-6-6-6--------|
   --7-7-7-7-7-7--5-7---|--7-7-7-7-7-7--5-7---|--7-7-7-7-7-7--5-7---|--7-7-7-7-7-7--5-7---|
   --7-7-7-7-7-7--------|--7-7-7-7-7-7--------|--7-7-7-7-7-7--------|--7-7-7-7-7-7--------|
   --5-5-5-5-5-5--------|--5-5-5-5-5-5--------|--5-5-5-5-5-5--------|--5-5-5-5-5-5--------|
```

D   A

```
|--7-7-7-7-7-7--------|--7-7-7-7-7-7--------|--5-5-5-5-5-5--------|--5-5-5-5-5-5--------|
|--7-7-7-7-7-7--5-7---|--7-7-7-7-7-7--5-7---|--5-5-5-5-5-5--------|--5-5-5-5-5-5--------|
|--7-7-7-7-7-7--------|--7-7-7-7-7-7--------|--6-6-6-6-6-6--------|--6-6-6-6-6-6--------|
|--5-5-5-5-5-5--------|--5-5-5-5-5-5--------|--7-7-7-7-7-7--5-7---|--7-7-7-7-7-7--5-7---|
                                             |--7-7-7-7-7-7--------|--7-7-7-7-7-7--------|
                                             |--5-5-5-5-5-5--------|--5-5-5-5-5-5--------|
```

E   A

```
|--9-9-9-9-9-9--------|--9-9-9-9-9-9--------|--5-5-5-5-5-5--------|--5-5-5-5-5-5--------|
|--9-9-9-9-9-9--7-9---|--9-9-9-9-9-9--7-9---|--5-5-5-5-5-5--------|--5-5-5-5-5-5--------|
|--9-9-9-9-9-9--------|--9-9-9-9-9-9--------|--6-6-6-6-6-6--------|--6-6-6-6-6-6--------|
|--7-7-7-7-7-7--------|--7-7-7-7-7-7--------|--7-7-7-7-7-7--5-7---|--7-7-7-7-7-7--5-7---|
                                             |--7-7-7-7-7-7--------|--7-7-7-7-7-7--------|
                                             |--5-5-5-5-5-5--------|--5-5-5-5-5-5--------|
```

Single Note Blues Rhythm

Here's a shuffle rhythm guitar progression consisting of all single notes. This pattern is a good example of a *riff*. The riff is outlined in the first measure. As the progression follows a 12-bar blues, the riff is transposed to each new chord. This example is also based around a I - IV - V chord change in the key of D (D - G - A). Once you have this progression down, try to create some of your own single note riff rhtyhms.

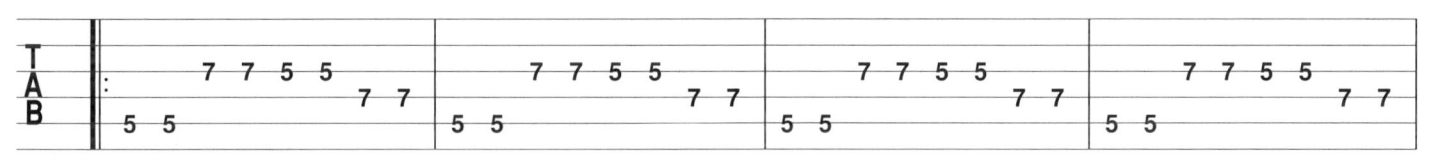

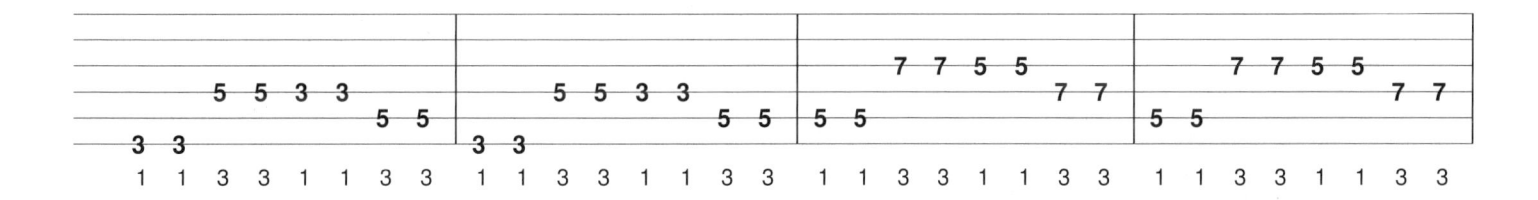

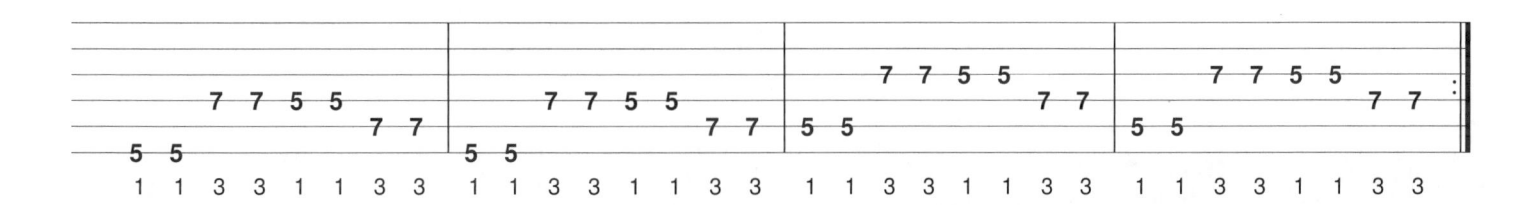

D

```
||:--------------------------|--------------------------|--------------------------|--------------------------|
   ----7--7--5--5-----------|----7--7--5--5-----------|----7--7--5--5-----------|----7--7--5--5-----------|
   --------------7--7--------|--------------7--7--------|--------------7--7--------|--------------7--7--------|
   -5--5---------------------|-5--5---------------------|-5--5---------------------|-5--5---------------------|
```

Fingering: 1 1 3 3 1 1 3 3   1 1 3 3 1 1 3 3   1 1 3 3 1 1 3 3   1 1 3 3 1 1 3 3

G   D

```
|--------------------------|--------------------------|--------------------------|--------------------------|
|----5--5--3--3-----------|----5--5--3--3-----------|----7--7--5--5-----------|----7--7--5--5-----------|
|--------------5--5--------|--------------5--5--------|--------------7--7--------|--------------7--7--------|
|-3--3---------------------|-3--3---------------------|-5--5---------------------|-5--5---------------------|
```

1 1 3 3 1 1 3 3   1 1 3 3 1 1 3 3   1 1 3 3 1 1 3 3   1 1 3 3 1 1 3 3

A   D

```
|--------------------------|--------------------------|--------------------------|--------------------------|
|----7--7--5--5-----------|----7--7--5--5-----------|----7--7--5--5-----------|----7--7--5--5-----------:||
|--------------7--7--------|--------------7--7--------|--------------7--7--------|--------------7--7--------|
|-5--5---------------------|-5--5---------------------|-5--5---------------------|-5--5---------------------|
```

1 1 3 3 1 1 3 3   1 1 3 3 1 1 3 3   1 1 3 3 1 1 3 3   1 1 3 3 1 1 3 3

Transposing the Minor Pentatonic Scale

You can solo over the single note blues rhythm by transposing the minor pentatonic scale to D. Each of the five positions can be moved to a different fret, allowing you to solo in any key anywhere on the fretboard. For instance, if you were to move all of the A minor pentatonic scale positions two frets (one whole step) higher, you would be playing in B.

The following chart shows the minor pentatonic scale in some popular keys, indicating where each position starts by fret. Choose a key from the left hand column and follow the chart across to see which fret each position starts on. Since an octave is only 12 frets, some positions can be played in two different places on the neck.

key	1st position	2nd position	3rd position	4th position	5th position
A	5th & 17th frets	8th fret	10th fret	12th fret & open	3rd & 15th frets
C	8th fret	11th fret	13th & 1st frets	3rd & 15th frets	6th & 18th frets
E	12th fret & open	3rd & 15th frets	5th & 17th frets	7th fret	10th fret
G	3rd & 15th frets	6th & 18th frets	8th fret	10th fret	13th & 1st frets
B	7th & 19th frets	10th fret	12th fret	14th & 2nd frets	5th & 17th frets
D	10th fret	13th & 1st frets	3rd & 15th frets	5th & 17th frets	8th fret
F	1st & 13th frets	4th & 16th frets	6th & 18th frets	8th fret	11th fret

CHAPTER 5

Lead Techniques

Slides

In the following example, slide from note to note without lifting your finger off the fretboard. The "S" above the staff indicates a slide and the line between the notes shows the direction of the slide (up or down the neck). If there is a slur connecting two or more notes, pick only the first note and slide directly to the next without picking. You can perform slides using any finger, but you'll probably use first and third finger slides more often. This exercise is played using the first position A minor pentatonic scale. After you get this down, try using the slide technique in other positions as well.

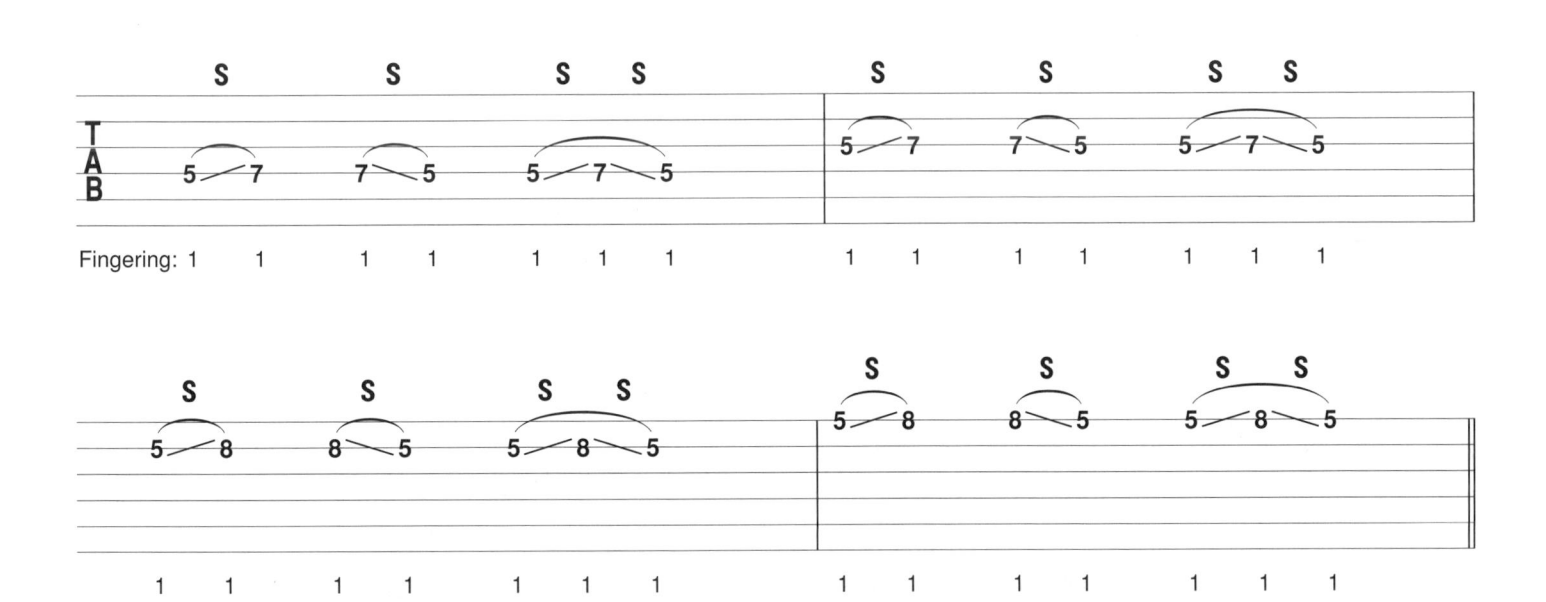

Vibrato

Vibrato is the small, fast shaking of a note. Vibrato is indicated by a squiggly line above the staff, extending out from a note. While sustaining a note, shake your finger slightly and "dig in" to the note to slightly vibrate the pitch and give it more expression. Vibrato can also be applied while bending.

45

Rockin' the Blues - Dead Strums

Here's a rock blues progression that incorporates dead strums, performed by muting the strings with your left hand and strumming the muted strings. These muted notes are shown using x's on the tab staff below. Pay attention to the picking symbols above the staff to show you when to upstrum or downstrum. This particular example places dead strums between most of the normal strums, giving the progression more of percussive sound and a rock feel. This example is also played in a shuffle feel. Jam along with the backing track until you have the groove, then try soloing over the progression using the A minor pentatonic scale in every position.

Blues Riffs That Will Make Yo Mama Scream Part 2

Now let's add another set of blues riffs to your bag of tricks. These riffs incorporate all of the lead techniques over several positions of the Am pentatonic scale. The last riff uses a double stop slide (sliding two notes at once). After mastering these riffs, try transposing them to other keys and positions on the fretboard.

Riff #1

Riff #2

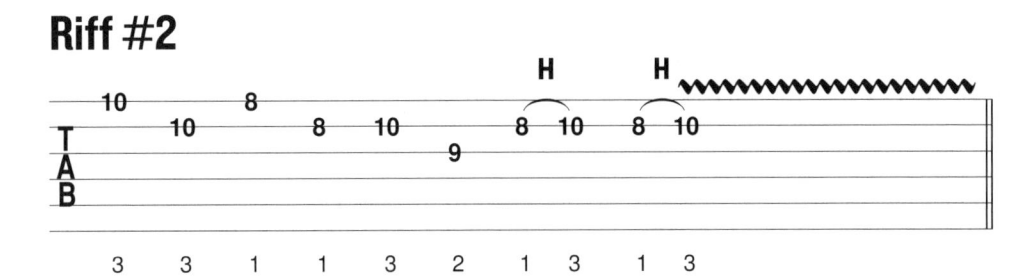

Riff #3

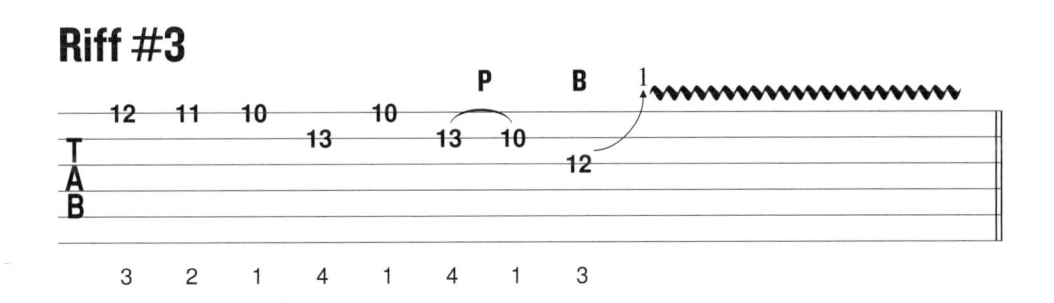

Riff #4

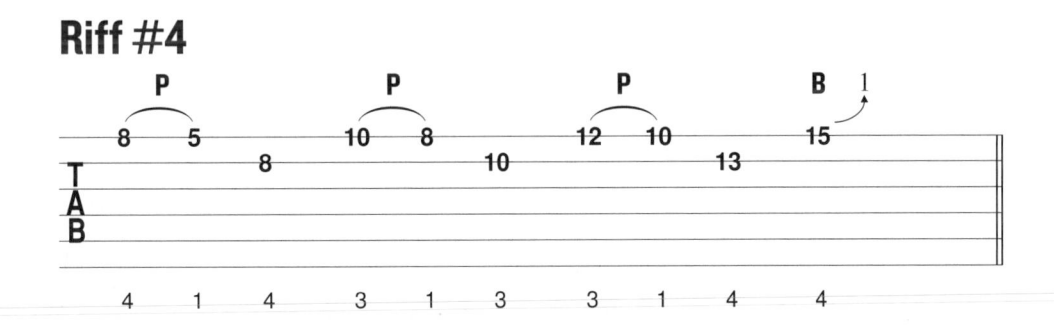

Riff #5

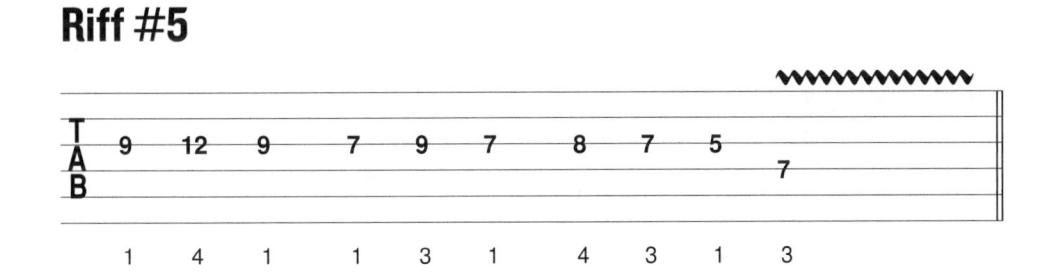

Riff #6

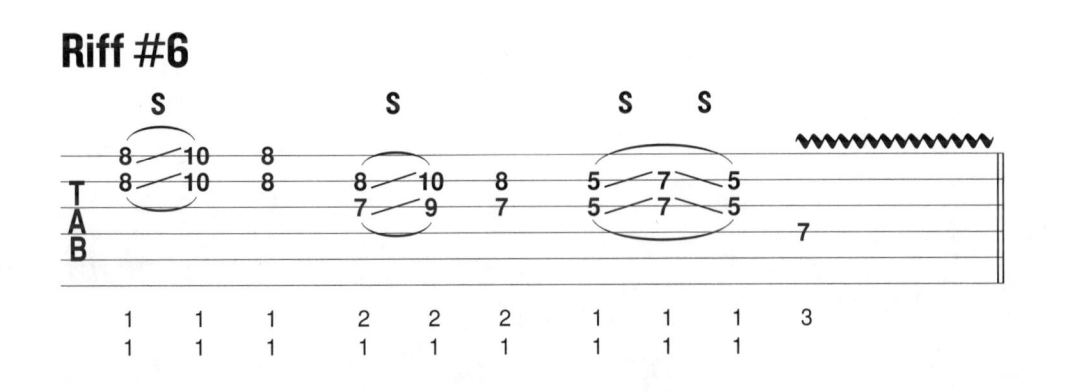

Open Chord Blues Progression in Em

The following progression uses some new open chord variations and suspensions. The chord diagrams show the fingerings for the chords used in this exercise. Notice that the fingering for the Em chord has been varied slightly in order to make it easier to change from chord to chord. Play along with the backing track and get the rhythm down. After you've learned the rhythm part, you can transpose the minor pentatonic scale positions to Em and solo over it. The five positions of the E minor pentatonic scale are also available on the Lesson Support Site. When creating your own solos, use bends, hammer ons, pull offs, slides and vibrato to add personal expression to your playing.

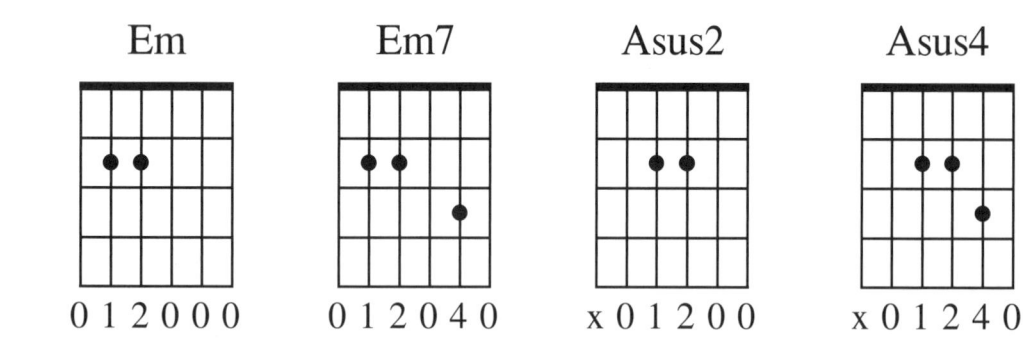

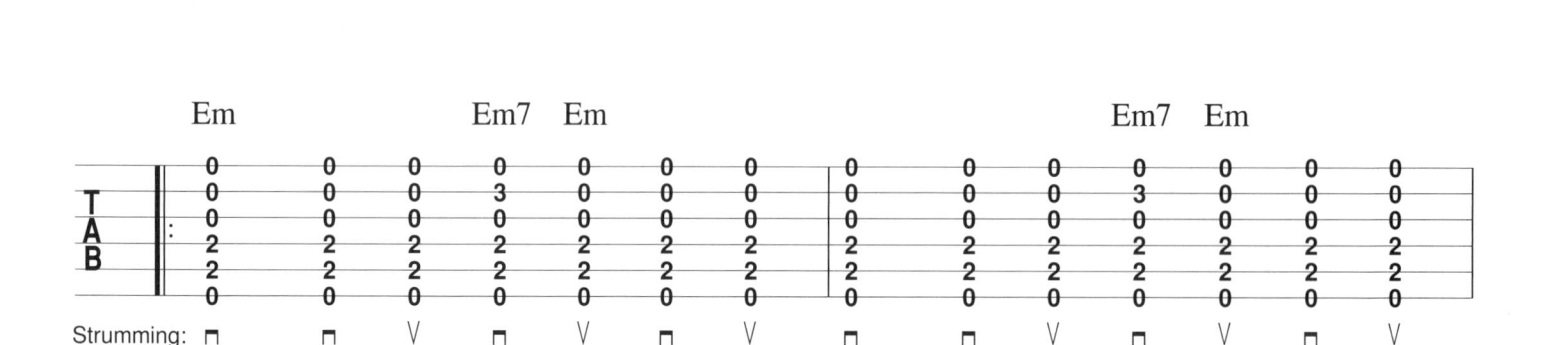

Em	Em7	Asus2	Asus4	B7
0 1 2 0 0 0	0 1 2 0 4 0	x 0 1 2 0 0	x 0 1 2 4 0	x 2 1 3 0 x

48

CHAPTER 6

Blues Scales - Key of E

The blues scale is a slight variation of the minor pentatonic scale. It contains one extra note between the 4th and 5th steps of the scale, called a *passing tone*. This particular passing tone is the flatted fifth of the scale, also known as the *blues tri-tone*. Using the blues tri-tone adds color and character to solos and riffs. This note is a chromatic passing tone because it passes from the 4th to the 5th steps of the scale in chromatic half steps. Passing tones are used to connect from note to note within a phrase and are generally not held for long durations.

The following five scale positions of the E blues scale are the same as the E minor pentatonic scale with the addition of the blues tri-tone. The x's in the scale diagrams to the right indicate where the blues tri-tones are played. Practice and memorize the E blues scale positions; we'll be using these scales to play solos in many of the following sections.

1st Position E Blues Scale

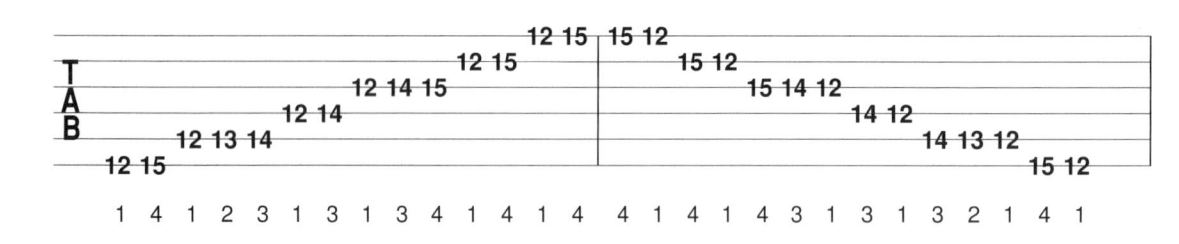

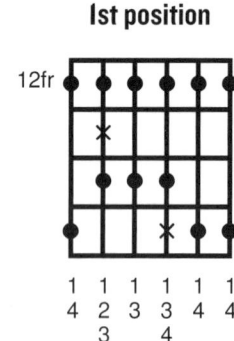

```
T |-----------------------------12-15-15-12-----------------------------|
A |-------------------------12-15---------15-12-------------------------|
  |---------------------12-14-15---------------15-14-12-----------------|
B |-----------------12-14-----------------------------14-12-------------|
  |------------12-13-14---------------------------------14-13-12--------|
  |--12-15----------------------------------------------------15-12-----|

  1 4  1  2  3  1  3  1  3  4  1  4  1  4  4  1  4  1  4  3  1  3  1  3  2  1  4  1
```

1st position

12fr

1 1 1 1 1 1
4 2 3 3 4 4
  3   4

2nd Position E Blues Scale

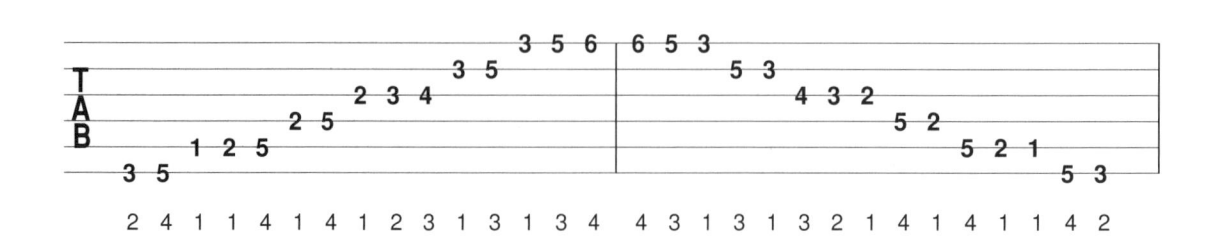

```
T |-------------------------3-5-6-6-5-3---------------------------------|
A |---------------------3-5-------------5-3-----------------------------|
  |-----------------2-3-4---------------------4-3-2---------------------|
B |-------------2-5---------------------------------5-2-----------------|
  |---------1-2-5-----------------------------------------5-2-1---------|
  |--3-5----------------------------------------------------------5-3---|

  2 4  1  1  4  1  4  1  2  3  1  3  1  3  4  4  3  1  3  1  3  2  1  4  1  4  1  1  4  2
```

2nd position

2 1 1 1 1
4 1 4 2 3 3
  4   3 4

50

3rd Position E Blues Scale

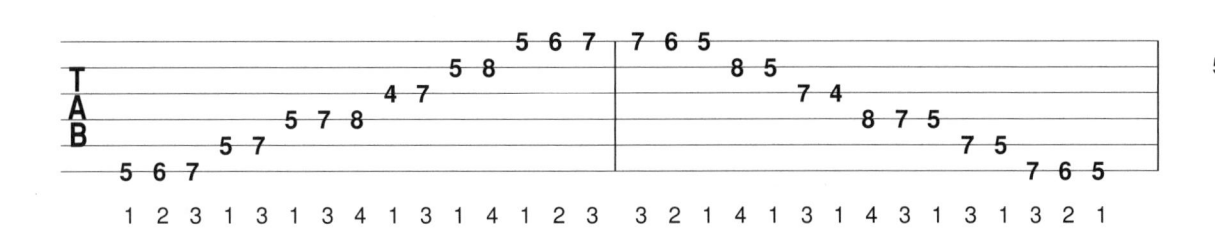

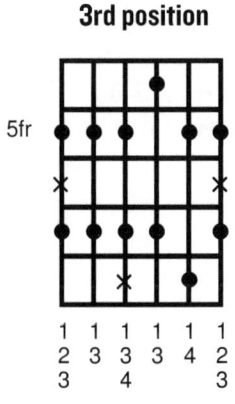

```
T|-----------------------5-6-7-|-7-6-5-----------------------|
A|-----------------5-8---------|-----------8-5---------------|
 |-------------4-7-------------|---------------7-4-----------|
B|---------5-7-8---------------|---------------------8-7-5---|
 |-----5-7---------------------|---------------------------7-5-|
 |-5-6-7-----------------------|-----------------------------7-6-5|

  1 2 3 1 3 1 3 4 1 3 1 4 1 2 3   3 2 1 4 1 3 1 4 3 1 3 1 3 2 1
```

3rd position
5fr

4th Position E Blues Scale

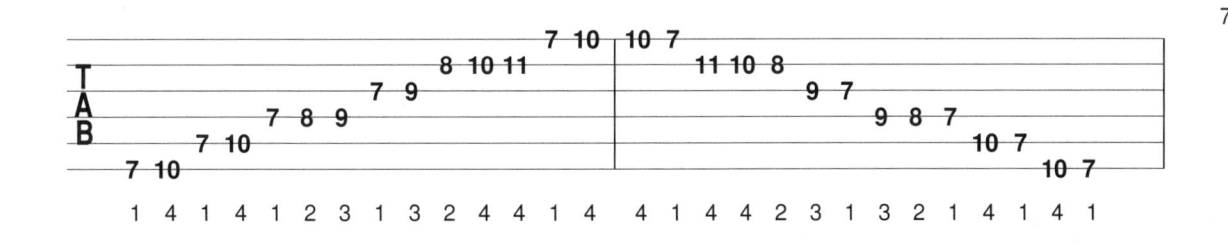

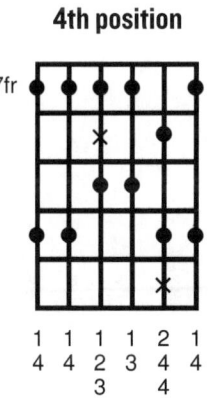

```
T|------------------------7-10-|-10-7------------------------|
A|-------------------8-10-11---|----11-10-8------------------|
 |--------------7-9------------|------------9-7--------------|
B|---------7-8-9---------------|---------------9-8-7---------|
 |----7-10---------------------|---------------------10-7----|
 |7-10-------------------------|---------------------------10-7|

  1 4 1 4 1 2 3 1 3 2 4 4 1 4   4 1 4 4 2 3 1 3 2 1 4 1 4 1
```

4th position
7fr

5th Position E Blues Scale

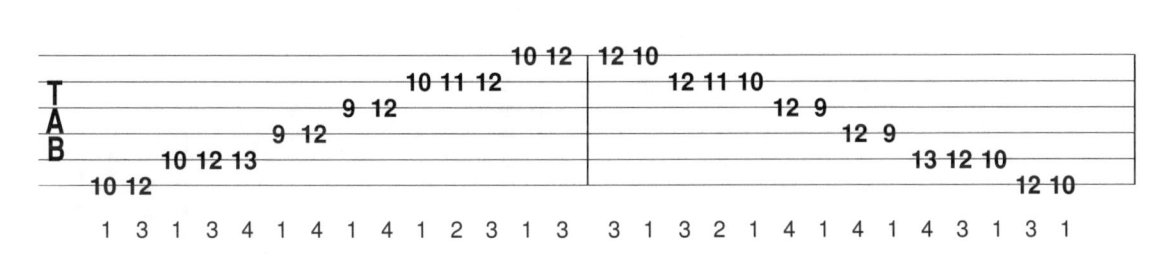

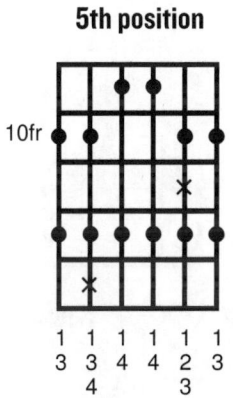

```
T|-------------------------10-12-|-12-10-------------------------|
A|-------------------10-11-12----|-------12-11-10----------------|
 |----------------9-12-----------|----------------12-9-----------|
B|---------10-12-13--------------|----------------------13-12-10-|
 |-10-12-------------------------|-----------------------------12-10|

  1 3 1 3 4 1 4 1 4 1 2 3   3 1 3 2 1 4 1 4 1 4 3 1 3 1
```

5th position
10fr

51

Open Position E Blues Scale

The first position of the E blues scale can also be transposed one octave lower and played in open position. This particular scale position is used often in blues music. Playing in open position makes hammer ons, pull offs and trills very easy to perform, making this particular scale a favorite for many guitarists. To play any scale position an octave higher or lower, move the scale pattern 12 frets in the appropriate direction.

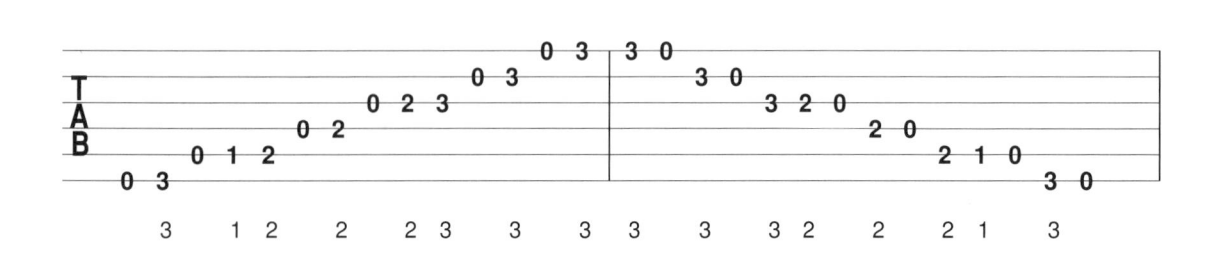

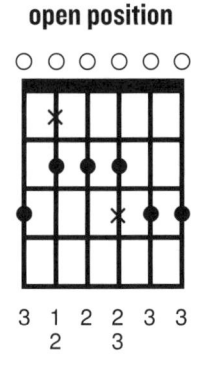

open position

```
T ─────────────────────────0─3─3─0─────────────────────────
A ───────────────────0─3───────────3─0───────────────────
A ─────────────0─2─3───────────────────3─2─0─────────────
B ────────0─2─────────────────────────────────2─0────────
  ──0─1─2─────────────────────────────────────────2─1─0──
  0─3────────────────────────────────────────────────3─0
  3   1 2   2   2 3   3   3 3   3 3 2   2   2 1   3
```

3 1 2 2 3 3
   2   3

Blues Scale Fretboard Diagram

The following fretboard diagram shows all of the notes in the E blues scales and how the positions overlap each other. The blues tri-tones are indicated by X's. Since the blues tri-tone is a passing tone within the minor pentatonic scale, the regular dots by themselves also indicate all of the notes of the E minor pentatonic scale. This is a very popular key for blues progressions and solos, so you should familiarize yourself with every position of the scale.

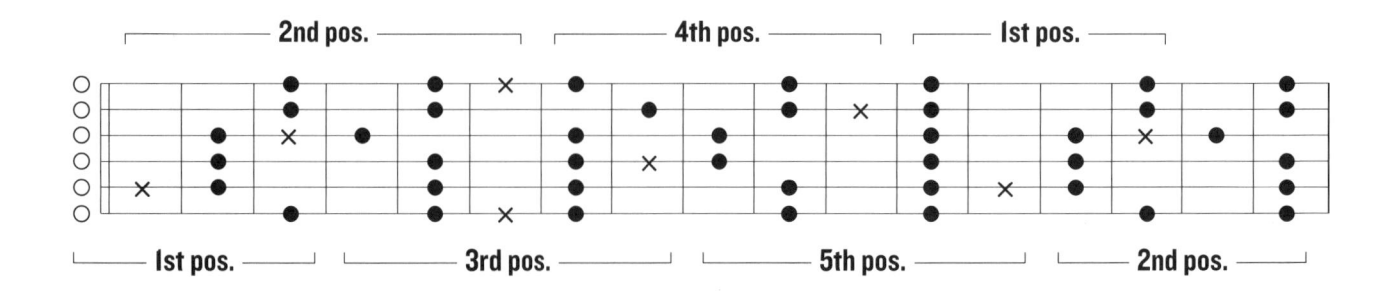

          2nd pos.   4th pos.   1st pos.

   1st pos.   3rd pos.   5th pos.   2nd pos.

Open String Blues Rhythm in E

The following rhythm is a standard I - IV - V progression in E with a shuffle feel. The last two measure phrase is a *turnaround* (a riff that brings you back around to the beginning of the progression). The riff should be played using alternate picking; let the notes ring out together. This particular turnaround uses a descending chromatic riff leading back to the V (five) chord, B. Practice the rhythm along with the backing track, then improvise and solo over it using the E blues scale in various positions.

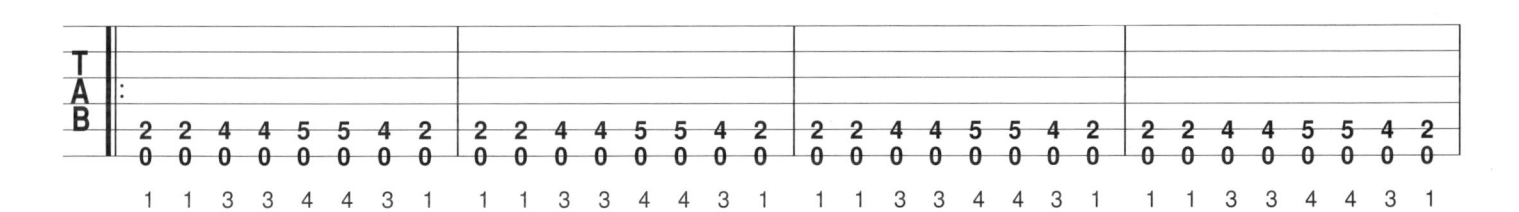

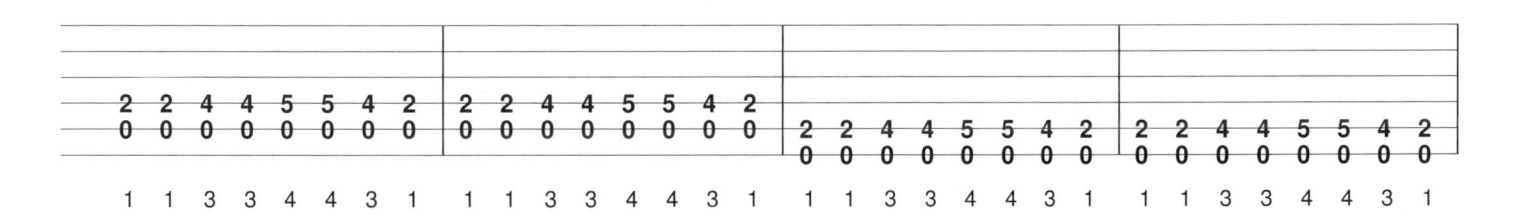

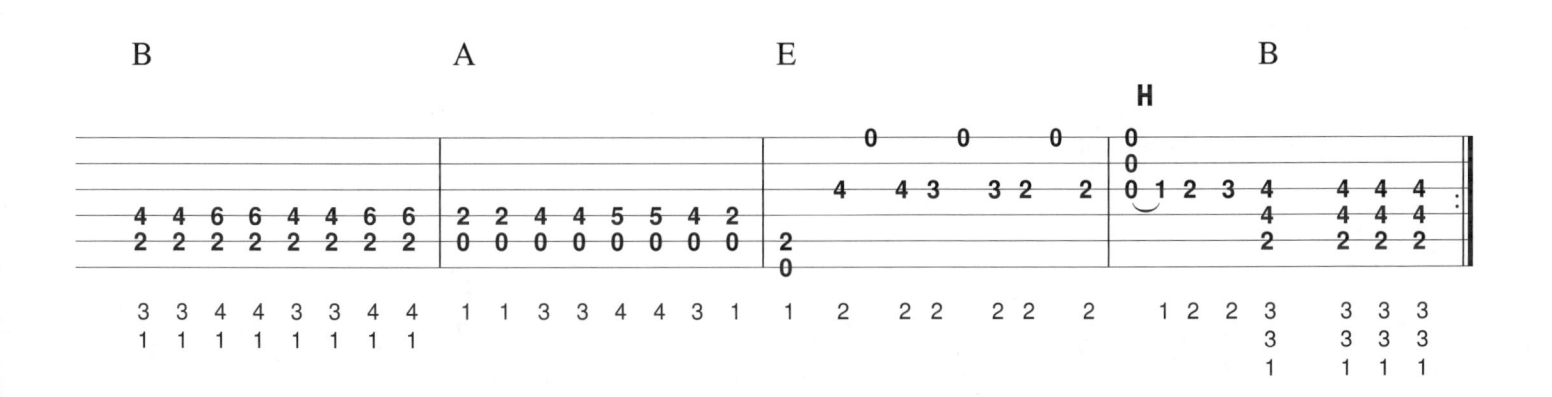

Advanced Bending Techniques

Half Step Bend

Half step bends are especially useful for soloing with blues scales. Train your ear to hear the difference between whole step and half step bends; eventually your fingers will instinctively know how much to bend the strings to achieve the correct pitches.

```
    1/2
T    7
A
B
     3
```

Ghost Bend

Ghost bends (sometimes referred to as pre-bends) are performed by bending the note to the proper pitch before striking the note. In this example, pre-bend the note a half step and then pick the note and gradually release the note to its original pitch.

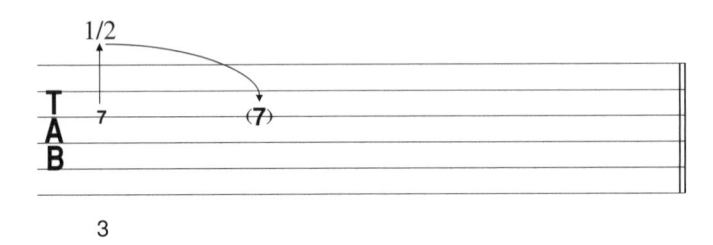

```
    1/2
T    7      (7)
A
B
     3
```

Double Pump Bend

You also bend and release the same note repeatedly without picking it again. The following example uses a bend-release-bend-release pattern. This technique can be used in a variety of ways.

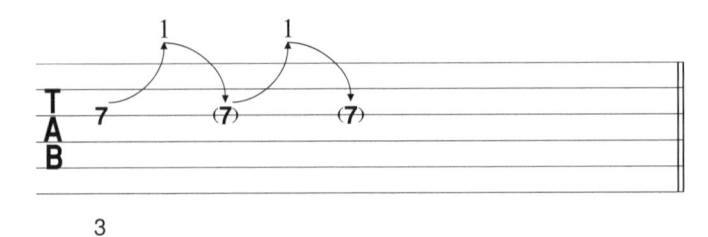

```
      1    1
T    7  (7) (7)
A
B
     3
```

Scream Bend

To perform the following scream bend, pick both notes simultaneously and bend just the lower note up a whole step. Keep the higher note stationary and allow it to ring out along with the bend.

```
          1
T    8
A    7
B
     4
     3
```

54

Blues Lead in E

Here's an example of a blues lead that can be played over the Open String Blues Rhythm in E from earlier in this section. Listen to the backing track to get the rhythm and the phrasing. This solo incorporates many different types of bends as well as hammer ons, pull offs, and slides.

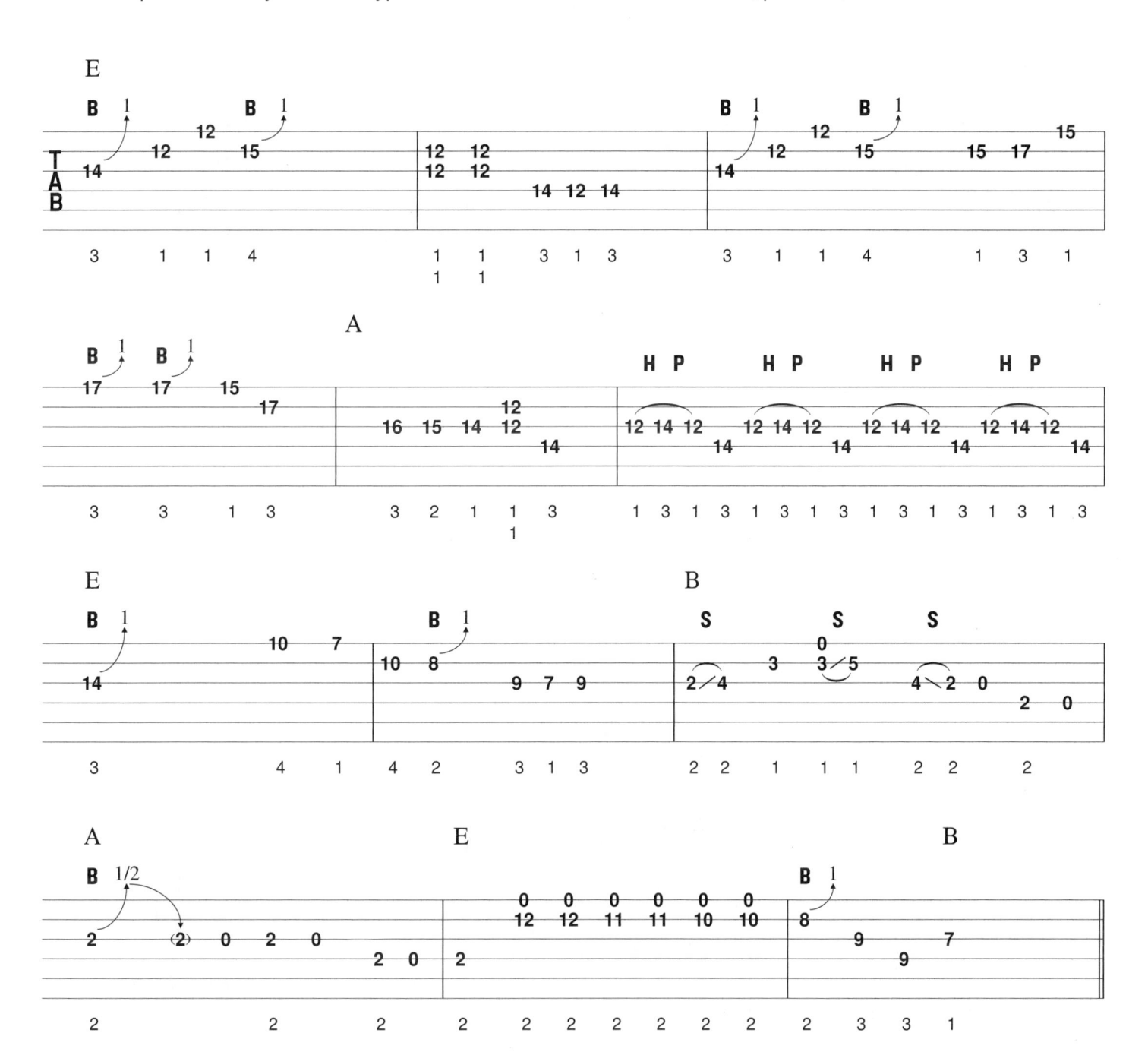

end of chapter 6

Congratulations! You've just completed all of the lessons on CD disc 1. The backing tracks for many of these lessons are included in the Music Minus One Backing Tracks at the end of each disc for you to practice along with. Before you continue to the next section, use your member number and log on to www.rockhousemethod.com to visit our online community. Review the additional information, take a quiz and test your knowledge. See you in the next section!

CHAPTER 7
Open Chords

Major Chords

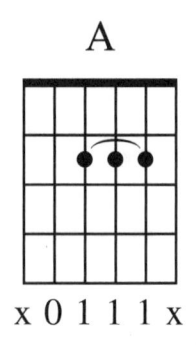

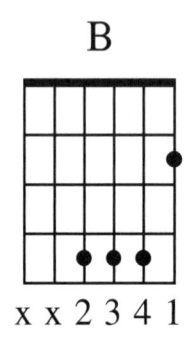

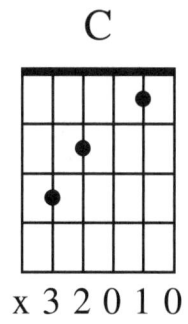

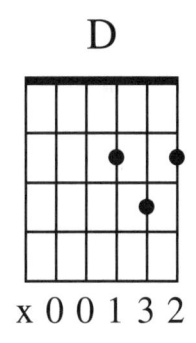

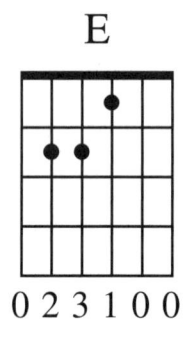

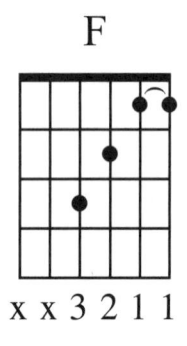

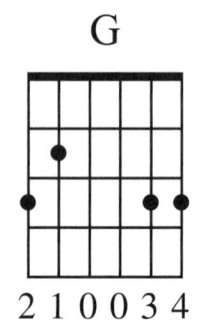

A
x 0 1 1 1 x

B
x x 2 3 4 1

C
x 3 2 0 1 0

D
x 0 0 1 3 2

E
0 2 3 1 0 0

F
x x 3 2 1 1

G
2 1 0 0 3 4

Minor Chords

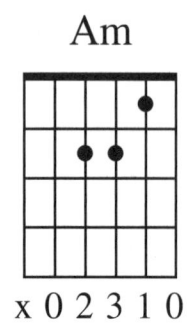

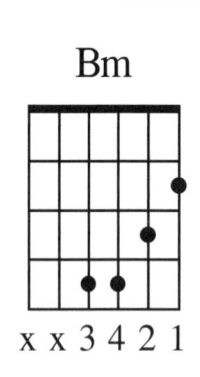

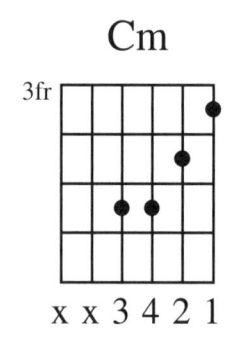

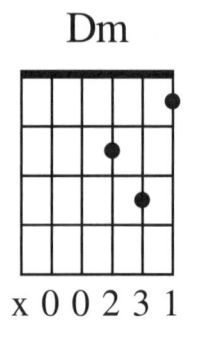

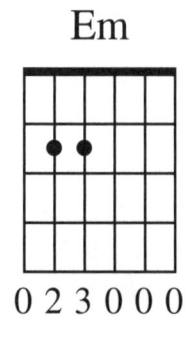

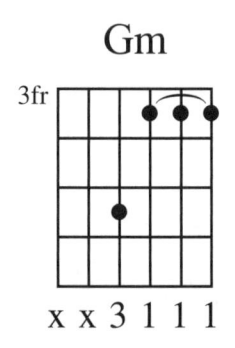

Am
x 0 2 3 1 0

Bm
x x 3 4 2 1

Cm
3fr
x x 3 4 2 1

Dm
x 0 0 2 3 1

Em
0 2 3 0 0 0

Fm
x x 3 1 1 1

Gm
3fr
x x 3 1 1 1

56

Advanced Blues Jazz Chords

The following chords are extensions of the regular major and minor chords. The 9th, major 7th and minor 7th chords are commonly used in blues to achieve a jazzier sound. These are all moveable chords and can be transposed to any key.

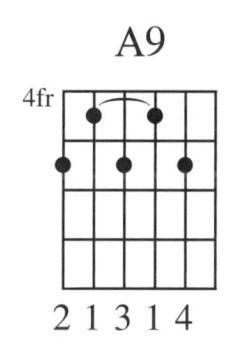

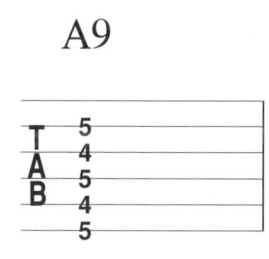

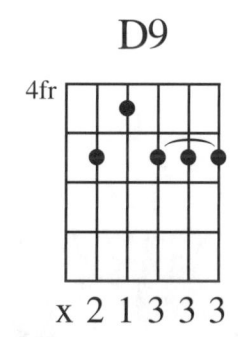

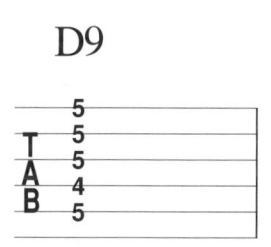

A9

4fr

2 1 3 1 4

A9

```
T  5
A  4
   5
B  4
   5
```

D9

4fr

x 2 1 3 3 3

D9

```
   5
T  5
A  5
   4
B  5
```

57

Am7

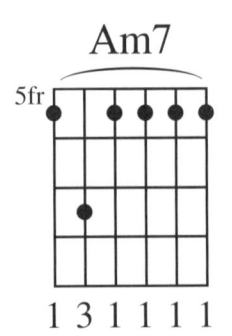

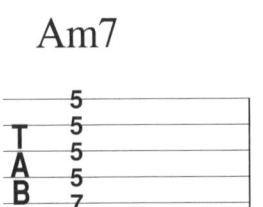

```
5fr
1 3 1 1 1 1
```

```
    5
T   5
A   5
B   5
    7
    5
```

Dm7

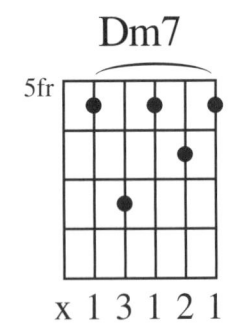

```
5fr
x 1 3 1 2 1
```

```
    5
T   6
A   5
B   7
    5
```

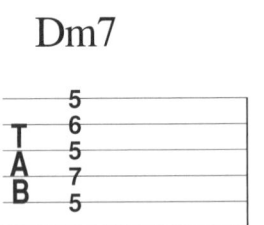

Amaj7

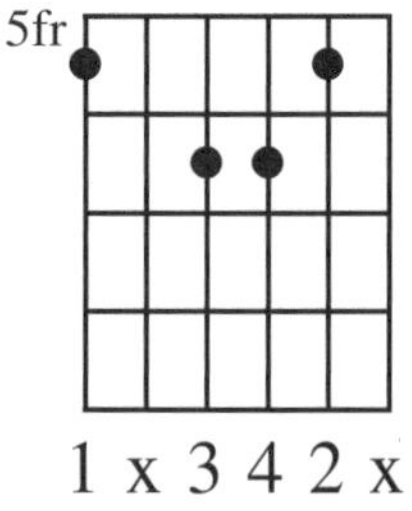

```
5fr
1 x 3 4 2 x
```

Amaj7

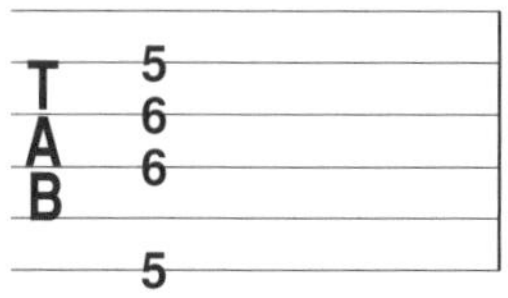

```
T 5
A 6
B 6
  5
```

Dmaj7

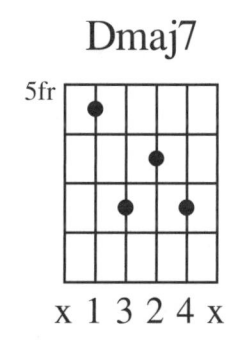

```
5fr
x 1 3 2 4 x
```

Dmaj7

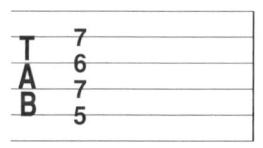

```
T 7
A 6
B 7
  5
```

59

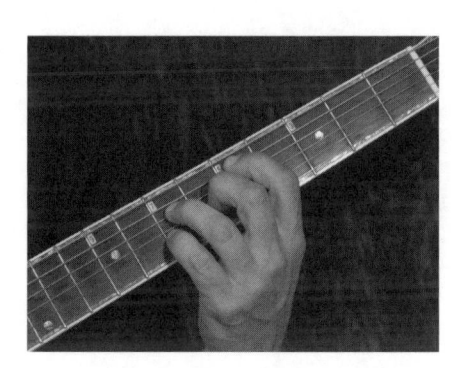

The Jazz Blues Fuze

This jazz blues fuze rhythm is another example of a 12-bar blues progression, the most popular progression used in blues music. This progression uses all 9th chords and is an example of a slow, jazzy blues. The rhythm is played with a straight feel in 6/8 time (six eighth notes per measure). The strumming pattern is indicated above the staff. Count along with the backing track to get the rhythm in your head. The rhythmic feel is in groups of three. Follow the slow blues drum beat and accent your strumming on the downbeats (the first and fourth eighth notes of each measure). When you get the feel down and you're ready to try soloing over the progression, transpose the blues scale positions to the key of A and use them to play leads along with the backing track.

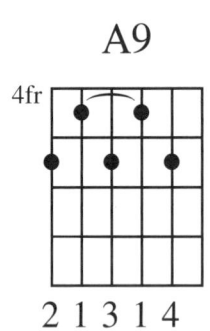

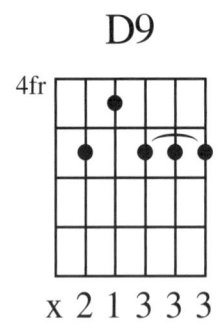

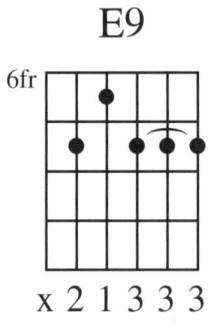

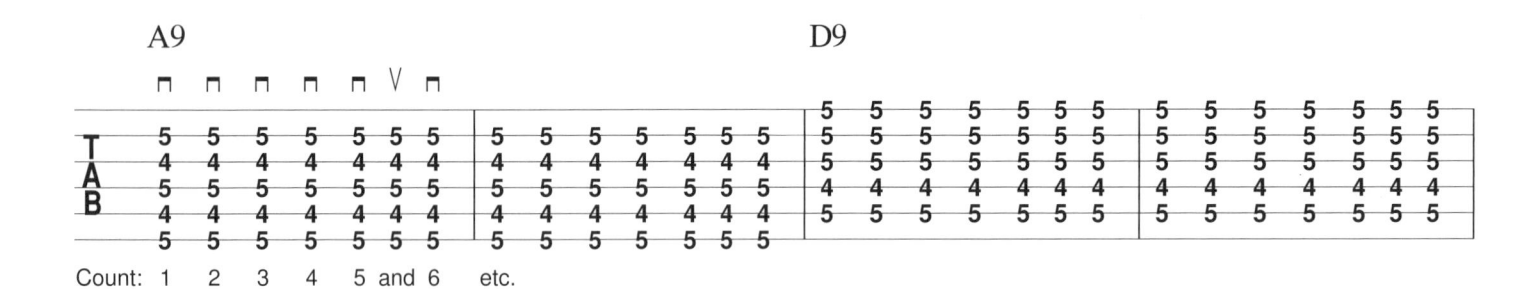

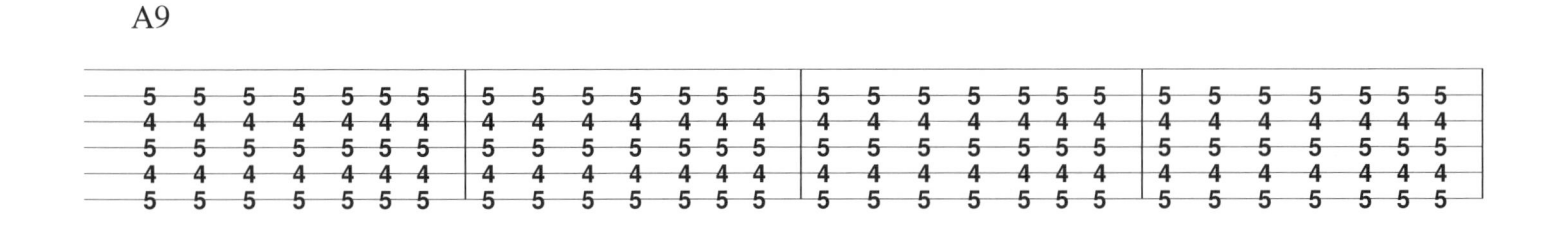

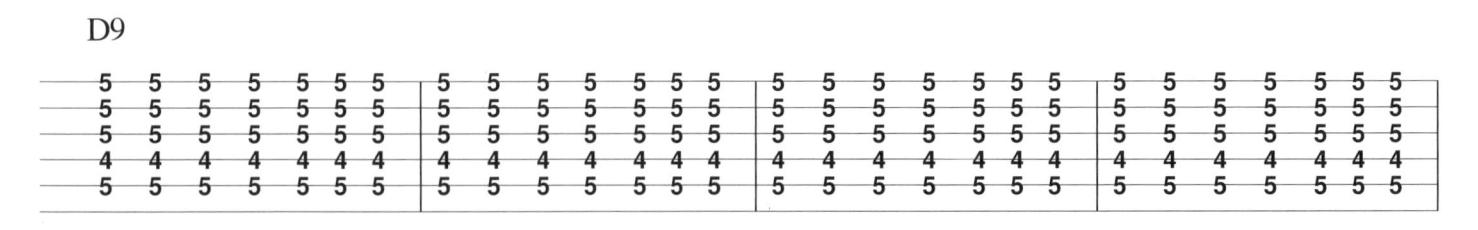

A9 — 4fr — 2 1 3 1 4

D9 — 4fr — x 2 1 3 3 3

E9 — 6fr — x 2 1 3 3 3

A9

```
⊓ ⊓ ⊓ ⊓ ⊓ V ⊓
```

| A9 | | D9 | |

Count: 1 2 3 4 5 and 6 etc.

A9

D9

Lead Techniques

Rakes

A rake is a series of muted adjacent strings picked before a note. Pick downward across the strings in one sweeping motion while deadening them with your left hand. In this example, the x's represent the rake leading into the notes on the 1st string. Rakes are commonly used to accent a bend.

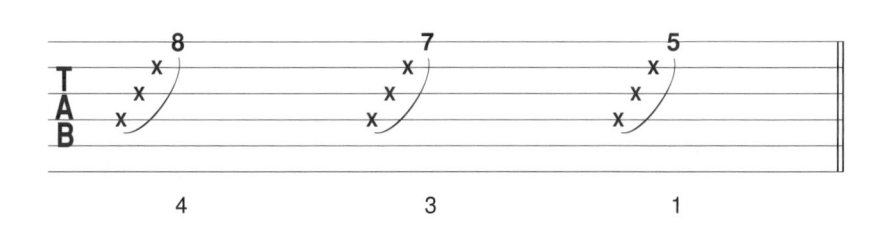

Pick & Finger

This technique is especially popular with blues and country players. Hold the pick as you normally would, then use your middle and ring fingers to pick additional notes. You can achieve quick jumps from low to high notes using this technique. In the first example, the notes are played together by downpicking with the pick and simultaneously plucking upward with the middle finger. Use a pinching motion with the pick and middle finger to pluck the notes together. The left hand fingering is indicated under the staff. Leave your first finger barred across the first three strings while reaching with your third and fourth fingers for the other notes along the 3rd string. Once you get the idea, try coming up with your own riffs and incorporate this style into your improvisational repertoire.

```
T|--12-----12-----12-----12-----12----||
A|--12-----14-----15-----14-----12----||
B|------------------------------------||

    1     1     1     1     1
    1     3     4     3     1
```

Here's another example using the pick and finger technique. The notes are picked individually in this exercise, alternating between the pick and middle finger. After the initial slide at the beginning of the riff, leave your second finger stationary at the 9th fret on the 3rd string. All of the notes on the 3rd string are downpicked using the pick. All of notes on the 1st and 2nd strings are plucked upward with the middle finger. After you have this technique down, try to use it in different scale positions and keys.

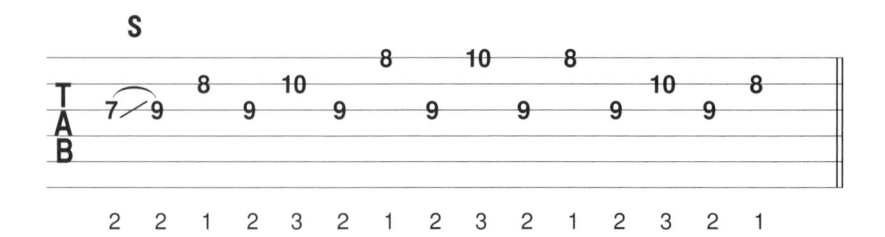

```
         S
                            8    10    8
                  8    10                  10    8
T|--7/9------9------9-----9----9----9------9-----||
A|-----------------------------------------------||
B|-----------------------------------------------||

    2  2  1  2  3  2  1  2  3  2  1  2  3  2  1
```

Advanced Blues Riffs

14-18 DISC 2

Now let's add some advanced blues riffs to your improvisational bag of tricks. These riffs are all recognizable and commonly used in blues solos and turnarounds. All five examples are shown here in the key of E. The first three riffs utilize the open strings, hammer ons, and pull offs.

In this first riff, all of the notes on the 3rd and 4th strings are fretted with the second finger or played open. This riff will develop coordination and help you to get comfortable using your second finger to perform slides and hammer ons.

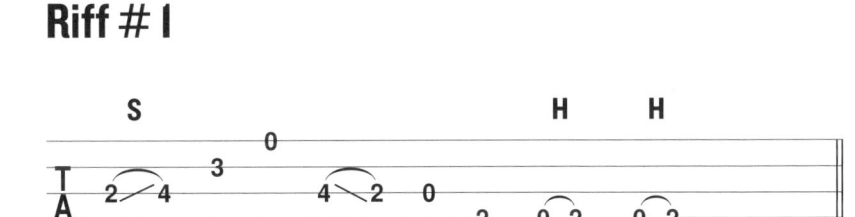

Riff #1

```
    S                           H     H
         0
    2/4  3      4\2  0
                      2    0 2   0 2

    2  2  1    2  2   2    2     2
```

The first part of this next riff is a *trill*. A trill is a fast series of hammer ons and pull offs. Pick the open string and then rapidly hammer on and pull off at the 2nd fret repeatedly. The last part of the riff is a half step bend at the 3rd fret of the 6th string, followed by the open 6th string. This 3rd fret bend and open string combination is a very popular move and is commonly used in almost all styles of music.

Riff #2

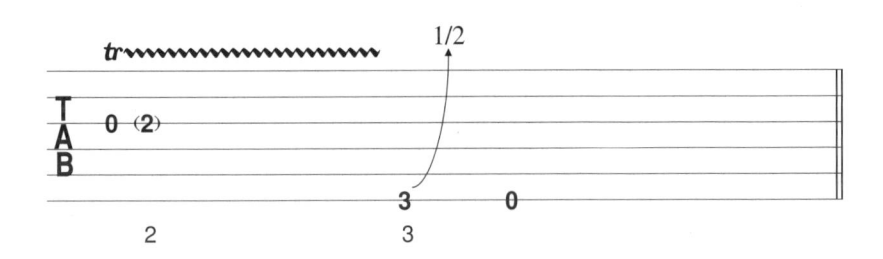

```
    tr~~~~~~~~~~~~~~       1/2
    0 (2)
                            3    0
      2                     3
```

63

The third advanced blues riff uses a series of pull offs to the open 1st string. This example demonstrates how you can use open string pull offs to jump quickly from position to position.

Riff # 3

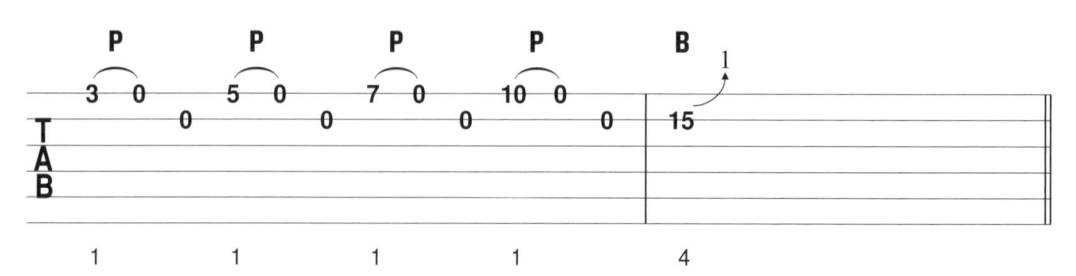

```
P       P       P       P        B
3  0    5  0   7  0   10  0      1
   0       0      0       0    15
                                  
                                  
                                  
1       1       1       1        4
```

The fourth riff descends through the notes of the E blues scale, followed by a 3rd fret half step bend and open 6th string combination.

Riff # 4

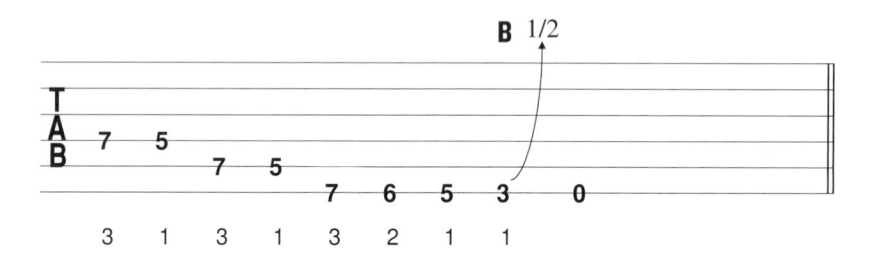

```
                                    B 1/2
                                    
 7  5
    7  5
       7  6  5  3      0
                       
 3  1  3  1  3  2  1   1
```

The last riff starts on a *unison* bend. Pick the notes together, bending the lower note until its pitch is in unison with the higher note. The next bend is a half step bend with the first finger at the 12th fret. Both of these bending techniques are very popular and widely used.

Riff # 5

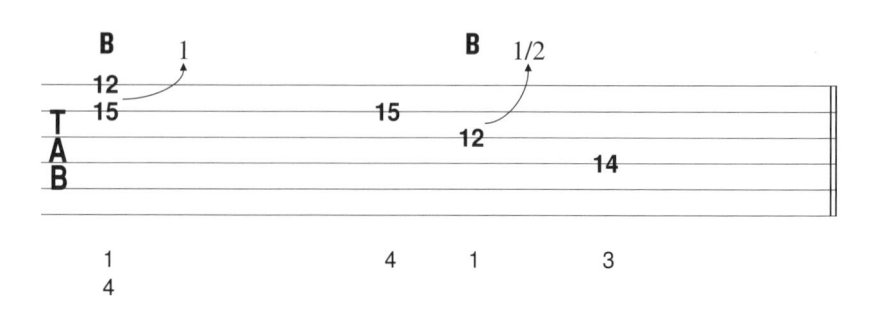

```
 B   1              B  1/2
12
15              15
                   12
                         14

1          4    1       3
4
```

64

Come visit us at one of our House of Blues Club venues where you can enjoy southern-inspired cuisine in our restaurant.

Experience an intimate fine dining, entertainment and lounge experience at the House of Blues Foundation Room.

CHAPTER 8
Barre Chords

6th String Barre Chords

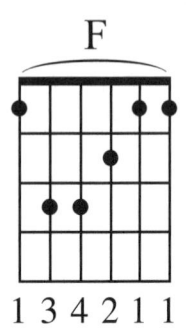

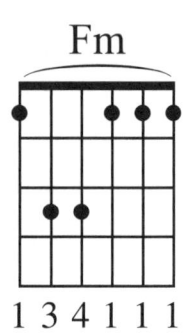

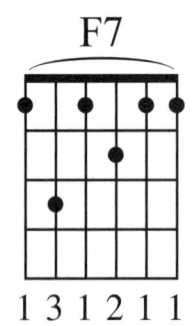

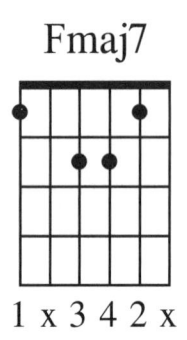

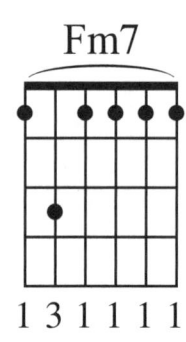

F
1 3 4 2 1 1

Fm
1 3 4 1 1 1

F7
1 3 1 2 1 1

Fmaj7
1 x 3 4 2 x

Fm7
1 3 1 1 1 1

5th String Barre Chords

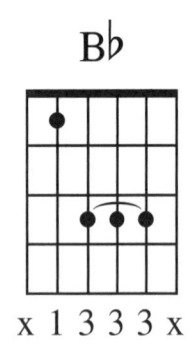

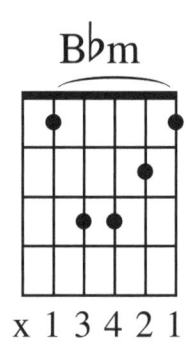

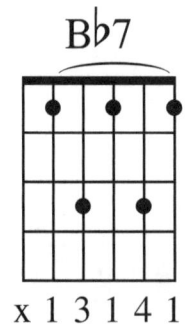

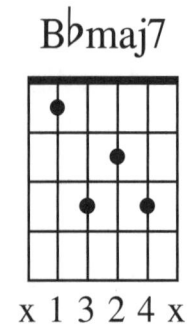

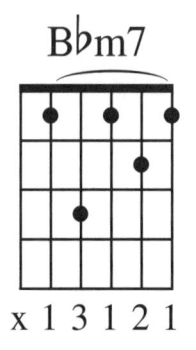

B♭
x 1 3 3 3 x

B♭m
x 1 3 4 2 1

B♭7
x 1 3 1 4 1

B♭maj7
x 1 3 2 4 x

B♭m7
x 1 3 1 2 1

Use the following chart to transpose the 6th and 5th string barre chords to any other fret.

6th string notes (F chord)	E	F	F#	G	G#	A	A#	B	C	C#	D	D#	E
fret number	Open	1	2	3	4	5	6	7	8	9	10	11	12
5th string notes (B♭ chord)	A	B♭	B	C	C#	D	D#	E	F	F#	G	G#	A

Skipping Strings

This is another blues technique using the pick and finger method. When fretting the notes, use your second finger for all of the notes along the 3rd string. Alternate between your pick and middle finger to pluck the notes. The riff is shown ascending and then descending. Try this technique at different speeds and in different rhythms.

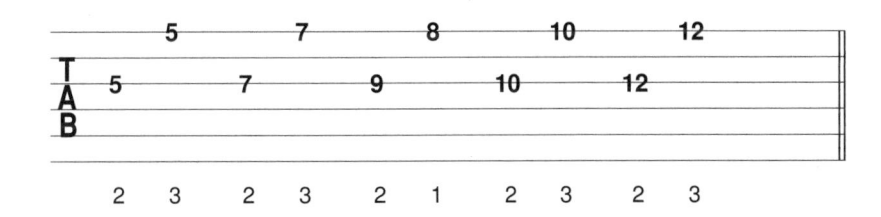

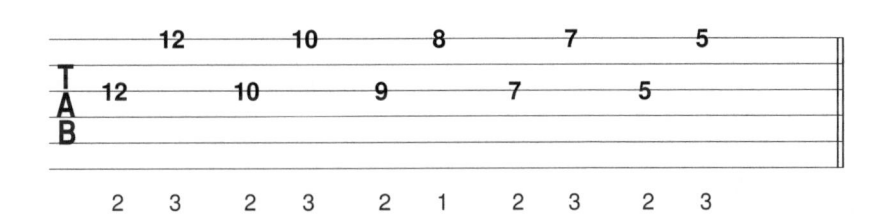

```
    ---5-----7-----8----10----12-----||
T---5-----7-----9----10----12--------||
A-----------------------------------||
B-----------------------------------||
    2  3  2  3  2  1  2  3  2  3
```

```
    --12----10-----8-----7-----5-----||
T---12----10-----9-----7-----5-------||
A-----------------------------------||
B-----------------------------------||
    2  3  2  3  2  1  2  3  2  3
```

67

The C Major Pentatonic Scale

The key of C major is the *relative major* to the key of A minor. A minor and C major are *relative keys* because they both contain the same notes. When playing in A minor, A is the root note; when playing in C major, C is the root note. The following 5 scale positions are the exact same scale fingerings as the A minor pentatonic scales from Chapter 2, however the root note is now going to be C. The root notes are circled on the tab staff, and are shown as open dots on the scale diagrams. Memorize where the root notes are in every scale position in order to solo in C major.

1st Position C Major Pentatonic Scale

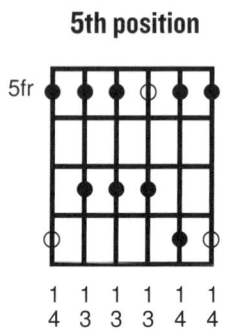

5th position, 5fr

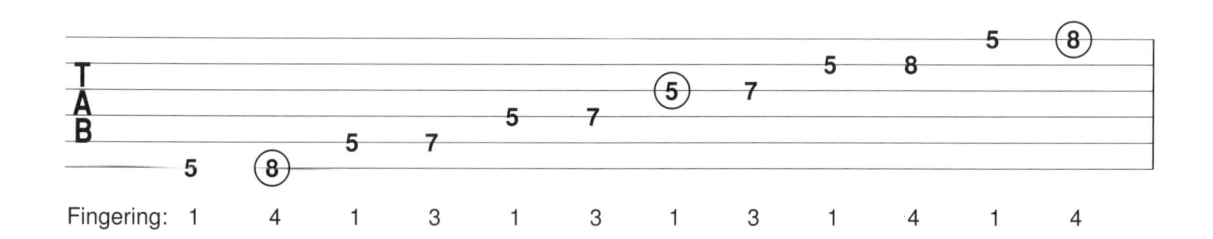

Fingering: 1 4 1 3 1 3 1 3 1 4 1 4

2nd Position C Major Pentatonic Scale

1st position, 8fr

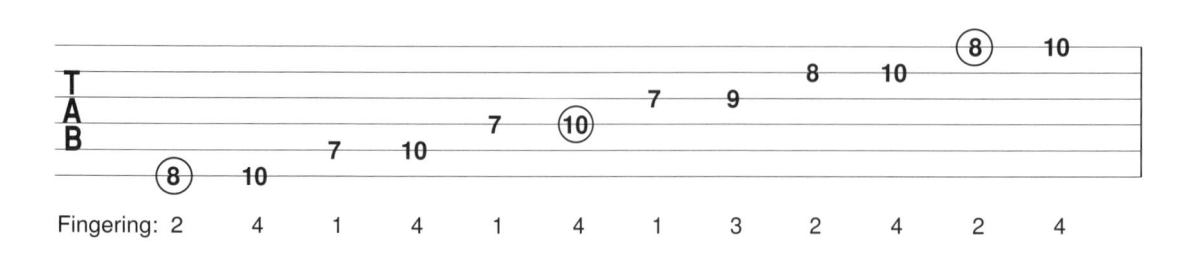

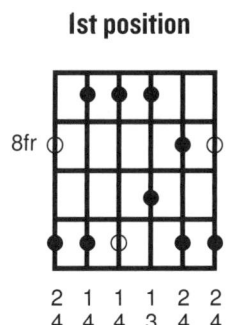

Fingering: 2 4 1 4 1 4 1 3 2 4 2 4

68

3rd Position C Major Pentatonic Scale

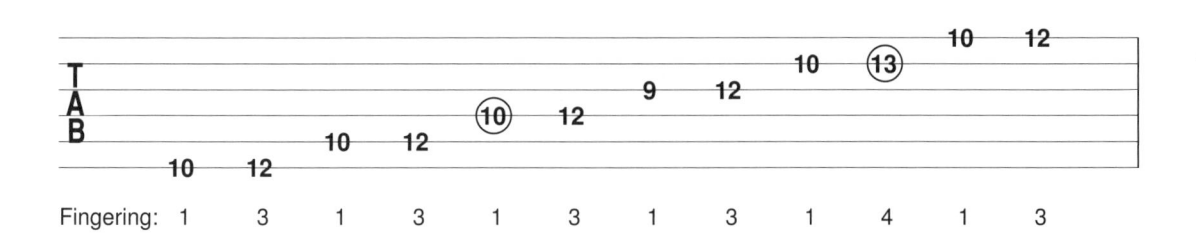

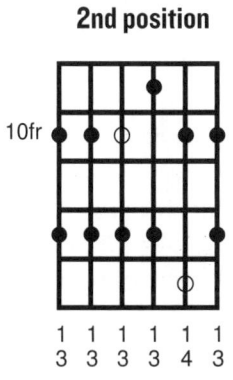

```
T |-----------------------------------------------10--12--|
A |-------------------------------9--12--10--(13)---------|
B |---------------(10)-12---------------------------------|
  |------10--12-------------------------------------------|
  |--10--12-----------------------------------------------|
  |-------------------------------------------------------|

Fingering:  1   3   1   3   1   3   1   3   1   4   1   3
```

2nd position
10fr
1 1 1 1 1 1
3 3 3 3 4 3

4th Position C Major Pentatonic Scale

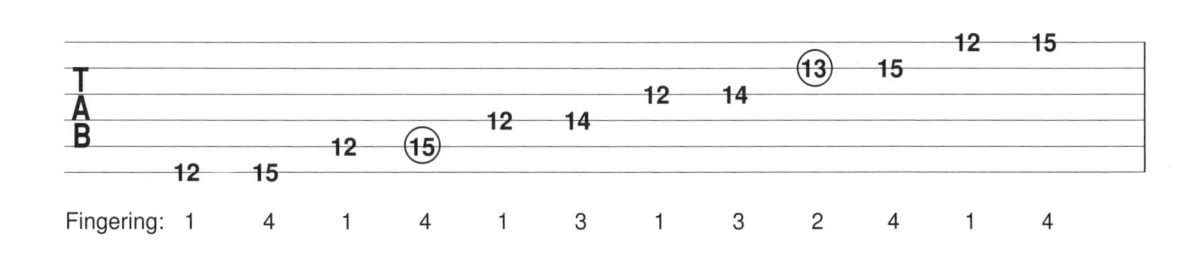

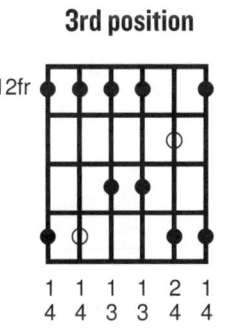

```
T |------------------------------------------12--15--|
A |-----------------------12--14--(13)--15-----------|
B |----------12--(15)--12--14------------------------|
  |--12--15------------------------------------------|

Fingering:  1   4   1   4   1   3   1   3   2   4   1   4
```

3rd position
12fr
1 1 1 1 2 1
4 4 3 3 4 4

5th Position C Major Pentatonic Scale

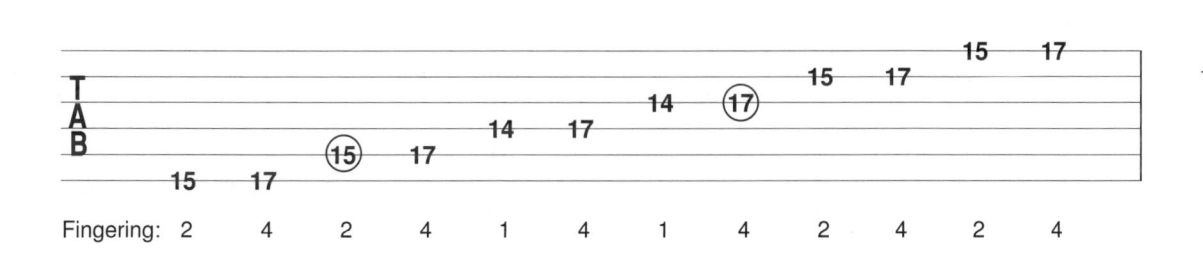

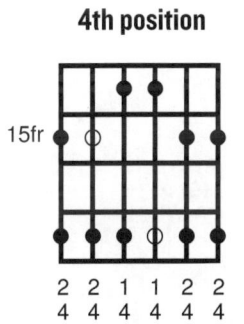

```
T |--------------------------------------15--17--|
A |-----------------------14--17--15--17---------|
B |--------(15)--17--14--17----------------------|
  |--15--17--------------------------------------|

Fingering:  2   4   2   4   1   4   1   4   2   4   2   4
```

4th position
15fr
2 2 1 1 2 2
4 4 4 4 4 4

69

Fast Blues in C (Sliding Rhythm)

This rhythm is a fast I - IV - V shuffle in C major. After learning this rhythm, you can solo along with the backing track using the C major pentatonic scales. The fingering is shown under the first staff; use the same fingering for the rest of the progression. When performing the slides and double-stops, lean your second finger downward slightly to deaden the string that's in between the two notes being played.

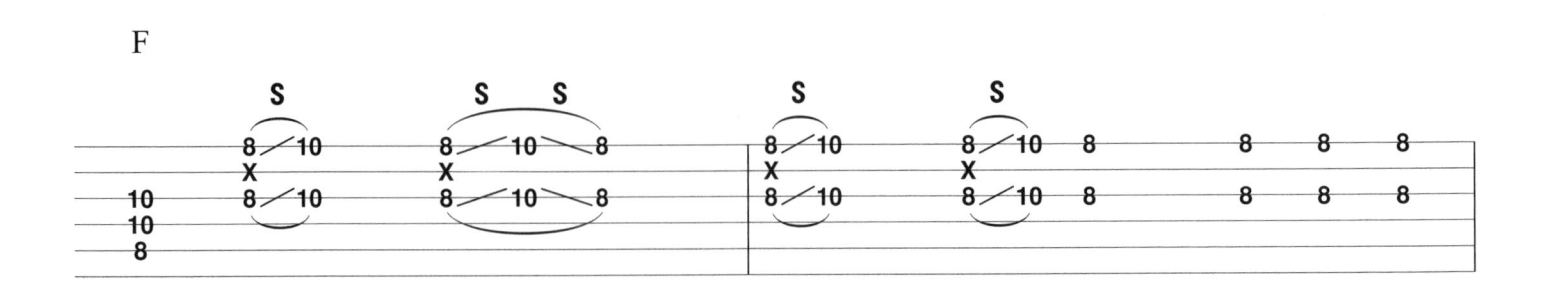

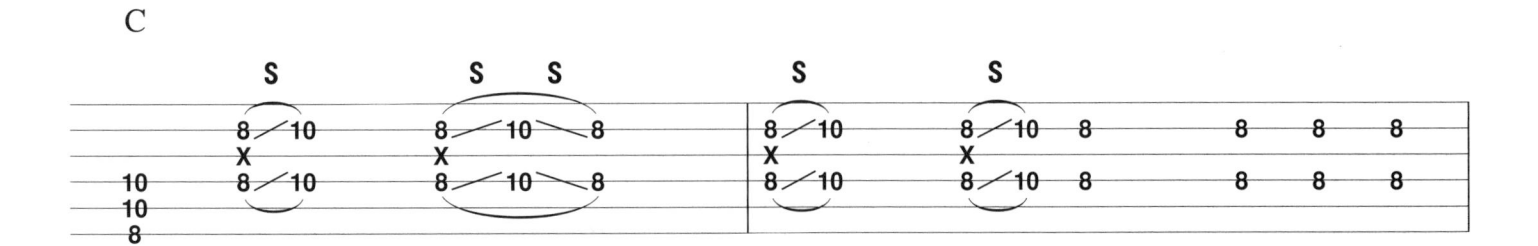

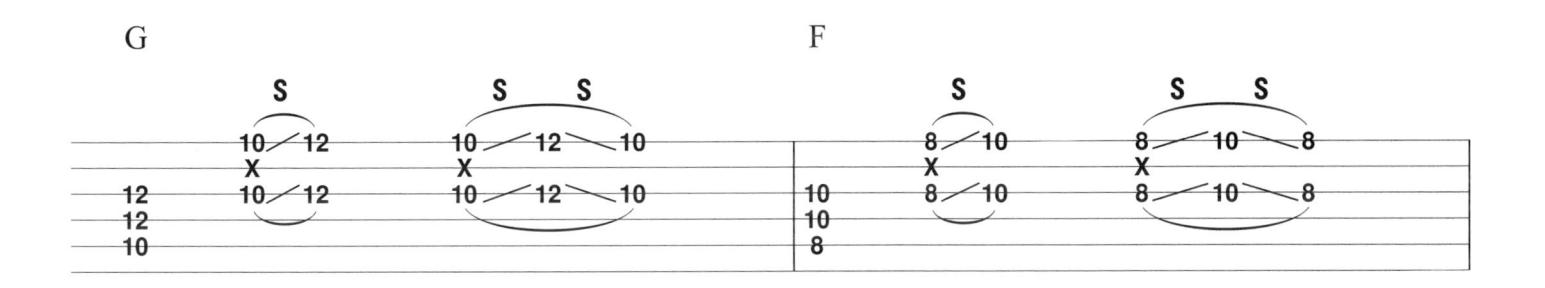

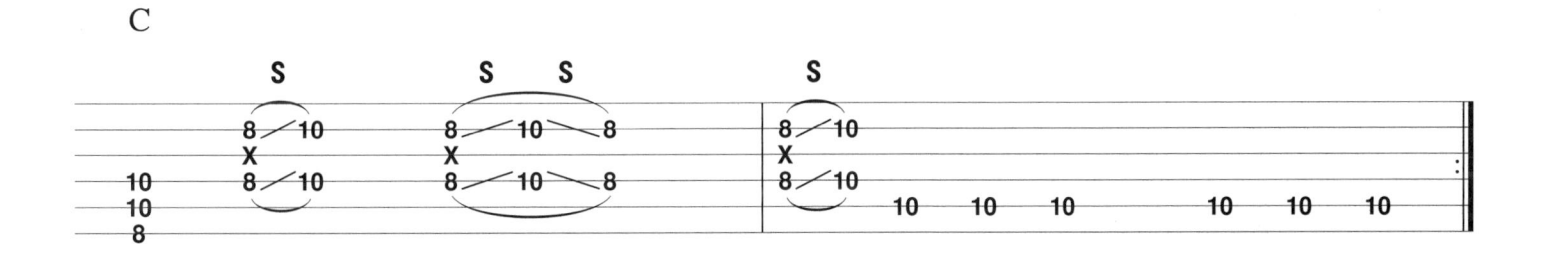

Quick Tip!

LEARN GRADUALLY AND HAVE REALISTIC GOALS

Don't try to play a lot of things you aren't ready for. Be realistic about your capabilities as a beginner and learn gradually. If you progress at a steady, methodical rate, your technique and control of the guitar will become solid as you advance. Strive to master each new technique, chord or scale before moving on to something else. Attempting things that you're not quite ready for can discourage you instead of inspire you to play.

Combining Major and Minor Scales

You can create a call and response effect by switching back and forth between the major and minor keys while soloing. Compare the two scale positions below. Notice that the finger pattern is the same for both scales; the major starts at the 5th fret, the minor starts at the 8th fret. The difference is in the placement of the root notes. This forms an easy way for you to swtich from major to minor just by moving the scale position three frets. To play a relative major pentatonic scale, you can move any of the minor pentatonic scale positions down three frets.

Try soloing over the Fast Blues in C from the previous section using both the major and minor pentatonics. You can solo for a few bars in major, then move three frets higher and solo in minor for a few bars to achieve a call and response effect. This is demonstrated on the DVD program to give you some ideas on how to use this technique.

C Major Pentatonic Scale

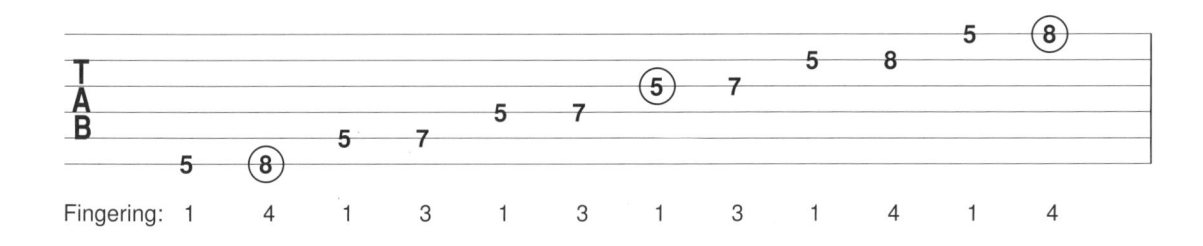

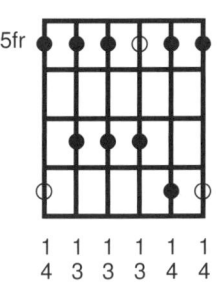

C Minor Pentatonic Scale

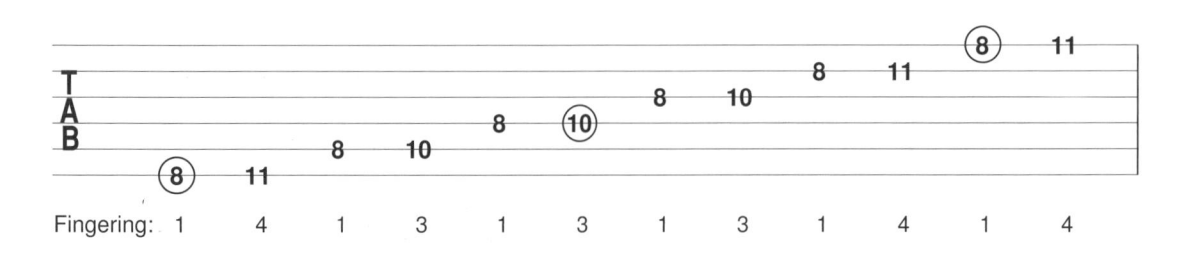

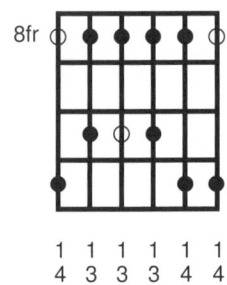

Improvisation Exercise

Many blues solos are created around the expansion of a main riff or phrase. You can take a simple, recognizable melody and keep coming back to it or play slight variations of it. This main theme gives the listener something to grasp on to in the same way as a chorus or hook does.

The melody below is shown in three different octaves on the guitar. Play over the same C major backing track and try working out a solo around this simple melody. You can play it anywhere within the progression; these themes work especially well when used in a turnaround. This technique is also demonstrated on the DVD. Once you understand the concept, try creating your own themes and melodies to build leads around.

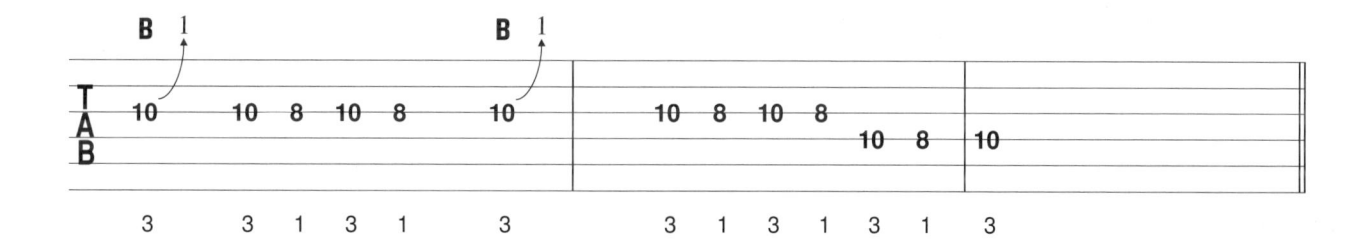

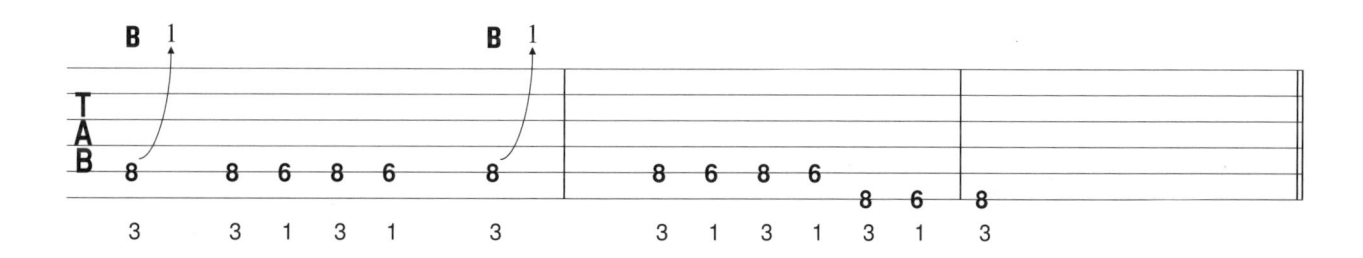

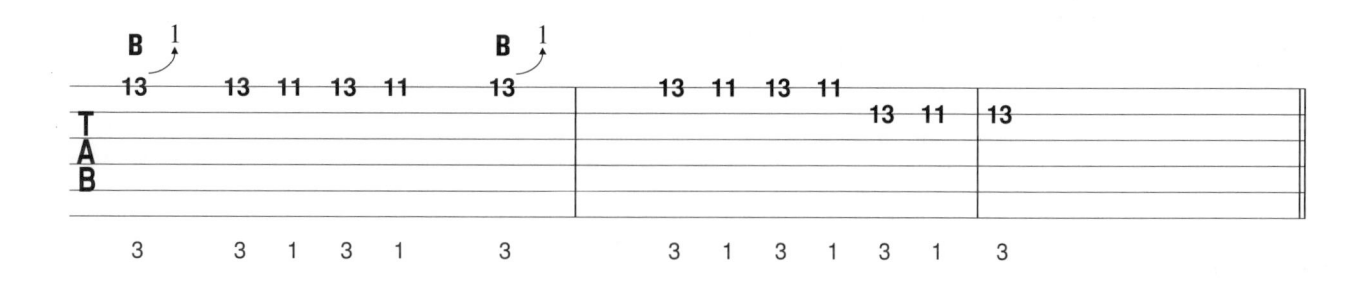

CHAPTER 9

Sixteenth Note Lead Pattern

Let's begin this section with a lead pattern designed to help build coordination and speed. Use a metronome and increase the tempo gradually over time. The pattern is intended to be played as sixteenth notes, with the bar lines placed after each group of four notes for reading convenience. The example below shows the pattern using a D minor pentatonic scale in the 1st position beginning at the 10th fret, ascending and descending.

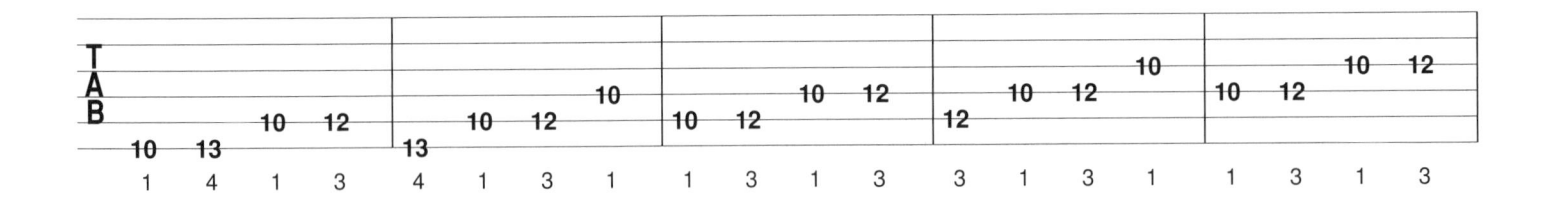

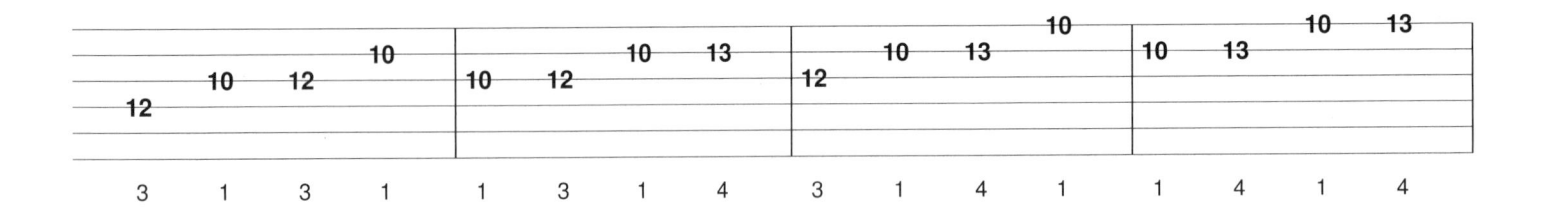

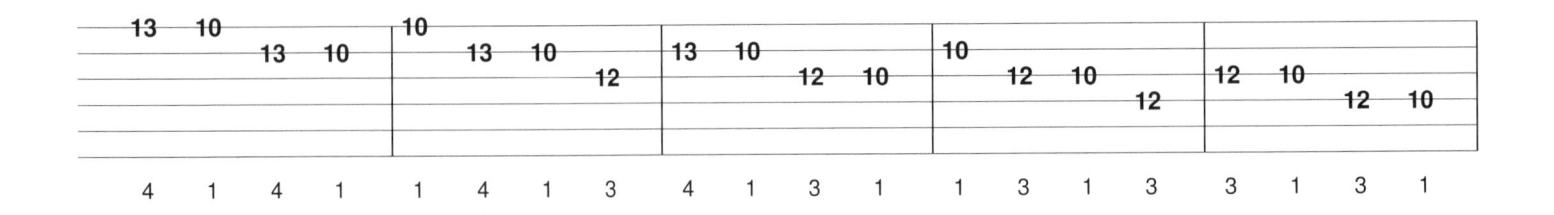

1st Position D Minor Pentatonic

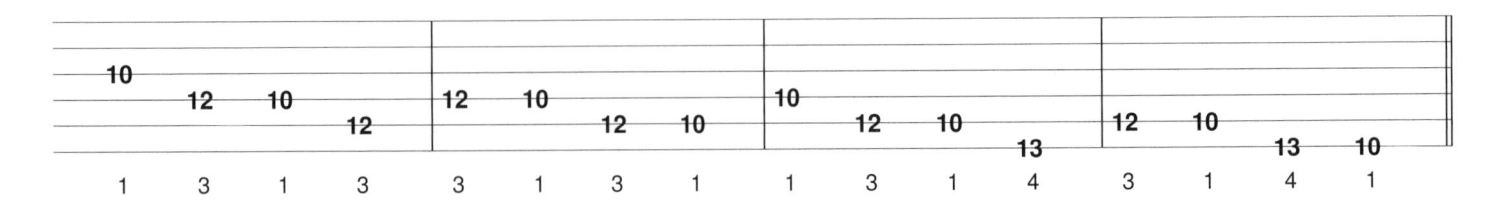

2nd Position D Minor Pentatonic

Here's the sixteenth note lead pattern using the D minor pentatonic scale in the 2nd position. Once you have the pattern memorized, transpose it to the remaining three scale positions. You can practice this pattern in any key or scale to help build strength and endurance.

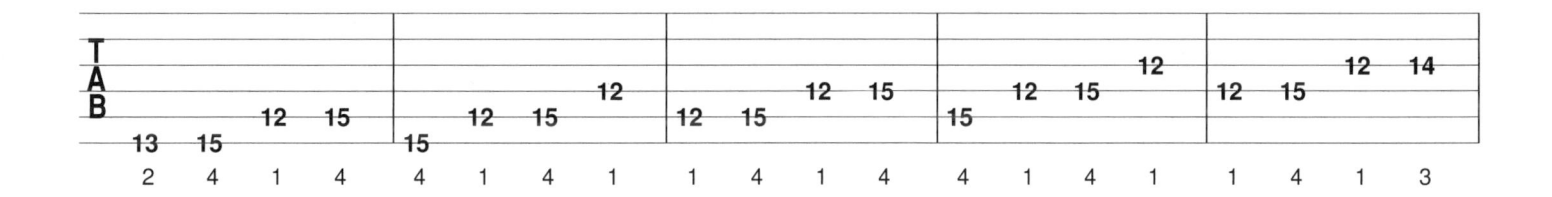

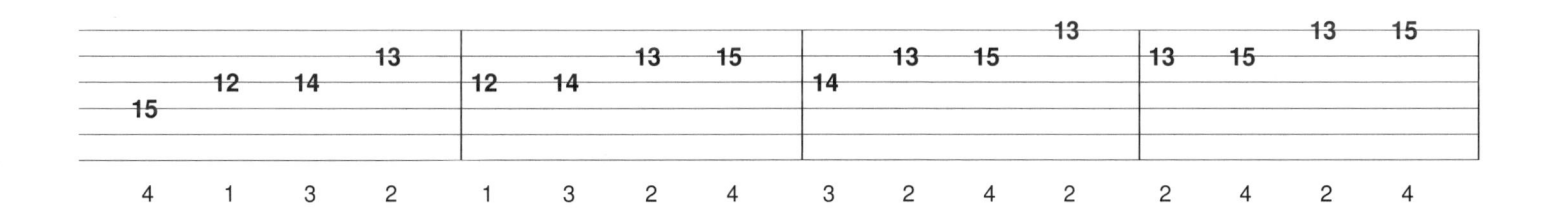

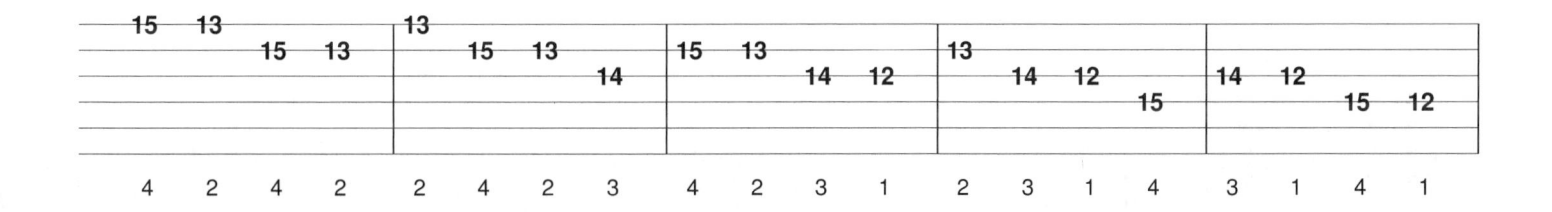

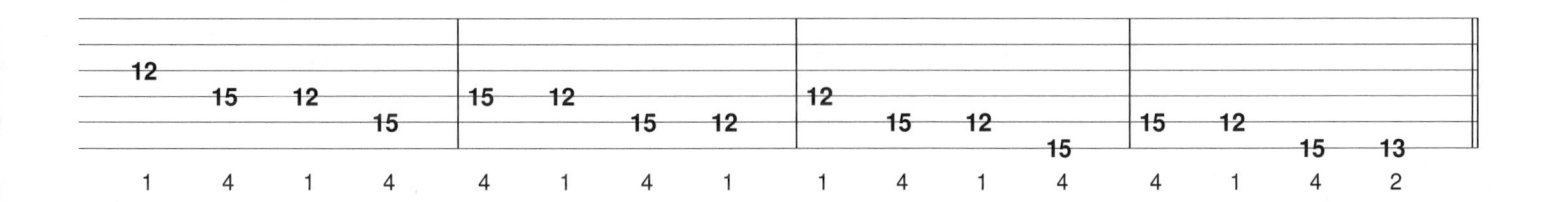

Blues Rock Progression - Key of D

The following blues rock progression in D is played using a sixteenth note rhythm. The chord changes are based on a I - IV - V progression with the addition of a repeated, single note riff placed between the chords. Use alternate strumming and picking to get the steady, sixteenth notes up to speed. The chords are all barre chords and are shown as full barre chords in the tab staff. You'll notice that these chords are not always fully strummed on the DVD program. This is a good example of interpretation and the use of performance techniques to spice up a simple progression. By varying the accents, muting, or how much of the chord your pick actually strums, you can add character to the sound and style.

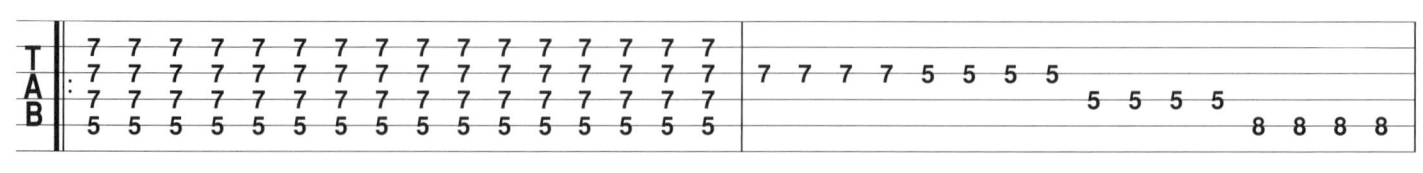

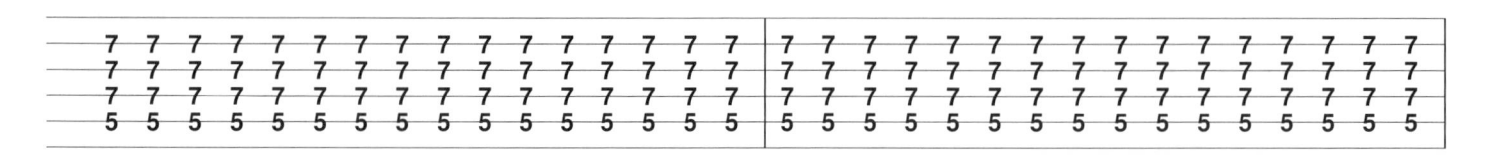

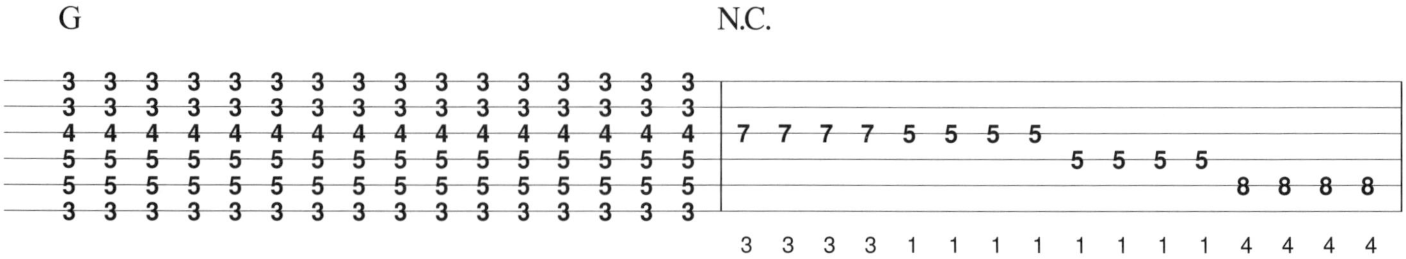

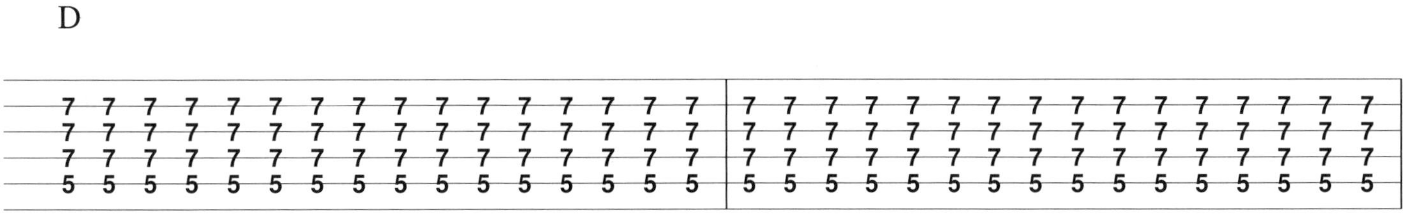

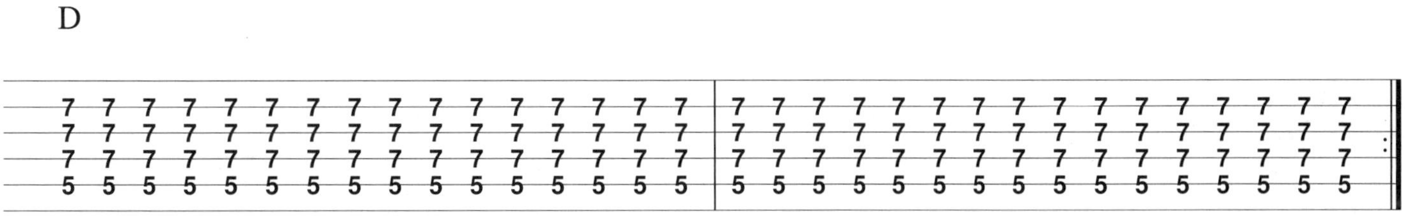

D

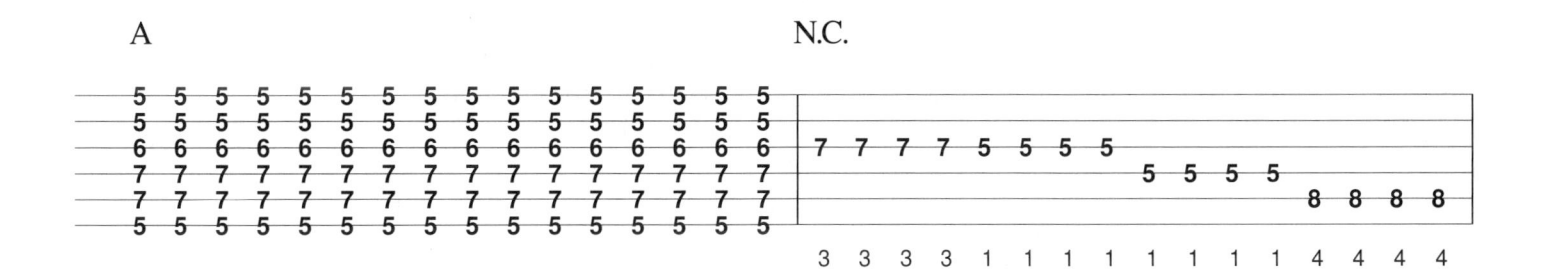

```
|-7-7-7-7-7-7-7-7-7-7-7-7-7-7-7-7-|-7-7-7-7-7-7-7-7-7-7-7-7-7-7-7-7-|
|-7-7-7-7-7-7-7-7-7-7-7-7-7-7-7-7-|-7-7-7-7-7-7-7-7-7-7-7-7-7-7-7-7-|
|-7-7-7-7-7-7-7-7-7-7-7-7-7-7-7-7-|-7-7-7-7-7-7-7-7-7-7-7-7-7-7-7-7-|
|-5-5-5-5-5-5-5-5-5-5-5-5-5-5-5-5-|-5-5-5-5-5-5-5-5-5-5-5-5-5-5-5-5-|
```

A   **N.C.**

```
|-5-5-5-5-5-5-5-5-5-5-5-5-5-5-5-5-|---------------------------------|
|-5-5-5-5-5-5-5-5-5-5-5-5-5-5-5-5-|---------------------------------|
|-6-6-6-6-6-6-6-6-6-6-6-6-6-6-6-6-|-7-7-7-7-5-5-5-5-----------------|
|-7-7-7-7-7-7-7-7-7-7-7-7-7-7-7-7-|-----------------5-5-5-5---------|
|-7-7-7-7-7-7-7-7-7-7-7-7-7-7-7-7-|-------------------------8-8-8-8-|
|-5-5-5-5-5-5-5-5-5-5-5-5-5-5-5-5-|---------------------------------|
                                    3 3 3 3 1 1 1 1 1 1 1 1 4 4 4 4
```

D

```
|-7-7-7-7-7-7-7-7-7-7-7-7-7-7-7-7-|-7-7-7-7-7-7-7-7-7-7-7-7-7-7-7-7-||
|-7-7-7-7-7-7-7-7-7-7-7-7-7-7-7-7-|-7-7-7-7-7-7-7-7-7-7-7-7-7-7-7-7-||
|-7-7-7-7-7-7-7-7-7-7-7-7-7-7-7-7-|-7-7-7-7-7-7-7-7-7-7-7-7-7-7-7-7-||
|-5-5-5-5-5-5-5-5-5-5-5-5-5-5-5-5-|-5-5-5-5-5-5-5-5-5-5-5-5-5-5-5-5-||
```

After you have the rhythm pattern and speed mastered, you can try playing leads along with the backing track using the D minor pentatonic scales. Practice soloing with the sixteenth note lead pattern in different positions, then create some of your own patterns. Fast sixteenth note rhythms aren't usually common in blues music, but they're used often in many rock styles. Blues techniques are often fused with other genres of music to create innovative new styles. Learning to play fast rhythms and leads in different musical styles is a great way to build coordination and strength in your picking hand, which will enable you to play clean and accurate leads at any tempo.

Classic Old School Blues Turnarounds

Here's a standard, old school blues progression in E. This shuffle rhythm uses riffs, seventh chords and turnarounds. Follow the strumming patterns and fingering references that are indicated above and below the tab staff when necessary.

The turnarounds and endings are underneath the repeat brackets at the end of each repetition. A blues turnaround is a riff at the end of a progression designed to lead smoothly back to the beginning of the rhythm. Blues endings are similar to turnarounds, but are used to conclude songs with a unique flair. Both turnarounds incorporate standard riffs that lead into the V chord (dominant). The final ending uses an open string pull off and hammer on combination riff that leads into the I chord (tonic). The use of dominant seventh chords in the turnarounds and ending give it that classic blues sound.

Once you have the rhythm down, try soloing over the backing track using the E blues scales from chapter 6. This is a great blues rhythm to practice all of the soloing techniques you've learned throughout the program.

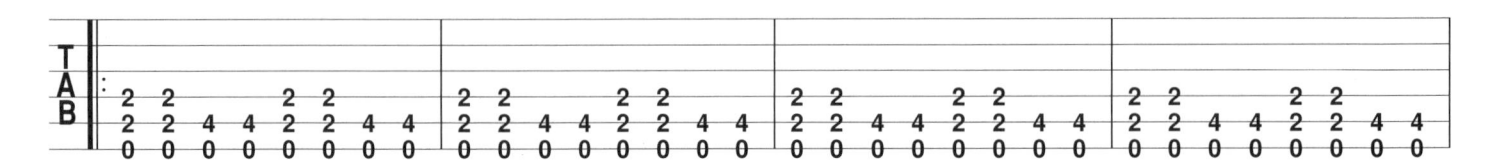

78

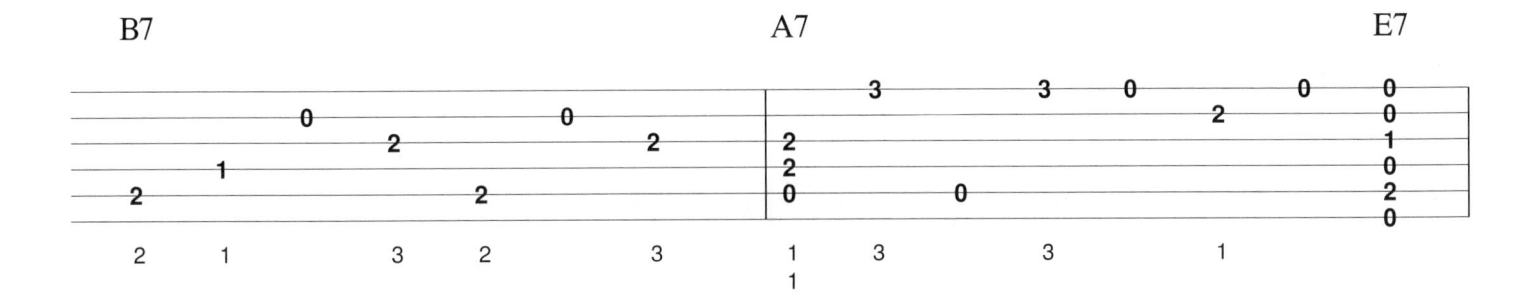

Turnaround #1

Turnaround #2

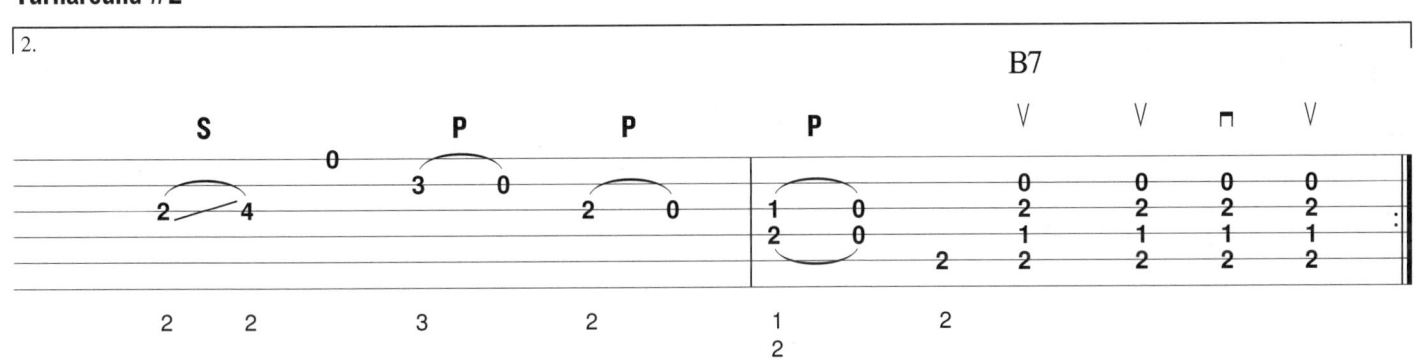

Ending

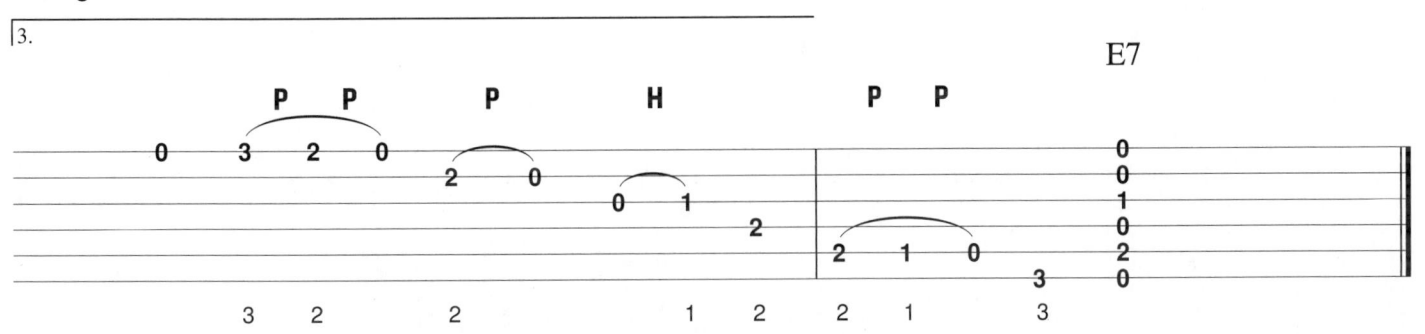

79

CHAPTER 10

Modern Blues Progression - Circle of Fourths

The following progression is a slow blues in the key of Am. The rhythm is counted in three's and each chord is *arpeggiated* (the notes of each chord are picked out separately). Finger and hold the chord in each measure and let its notes ring out together. Follow the finger numbers under the tab staff to show you the proper chord fingerings. Play along with the backing track and practice the rhythm's slow ballad feel. The chord change progresses in a pattern of fourths; the distance from one chord to the next is the interval of a fourth. This is a common change that is also used in many musical styles ranging from classical to metal.

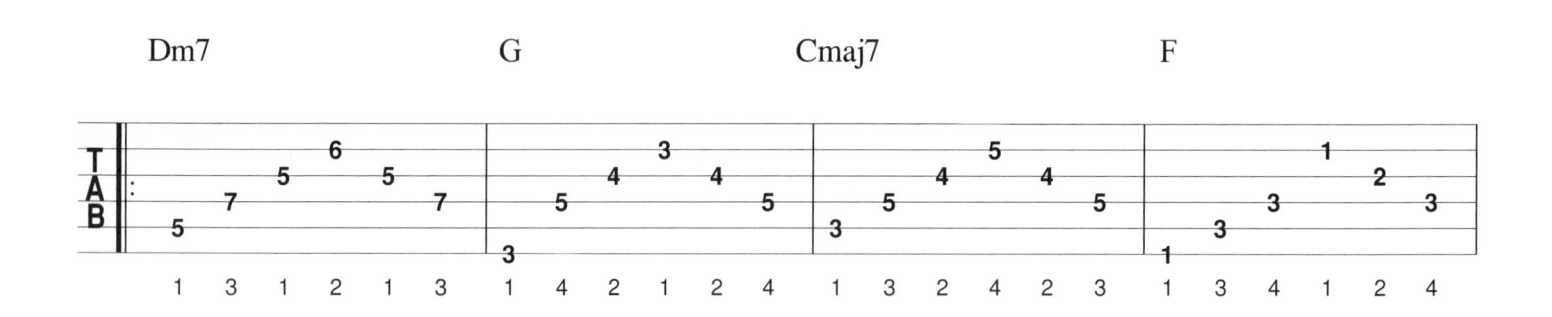

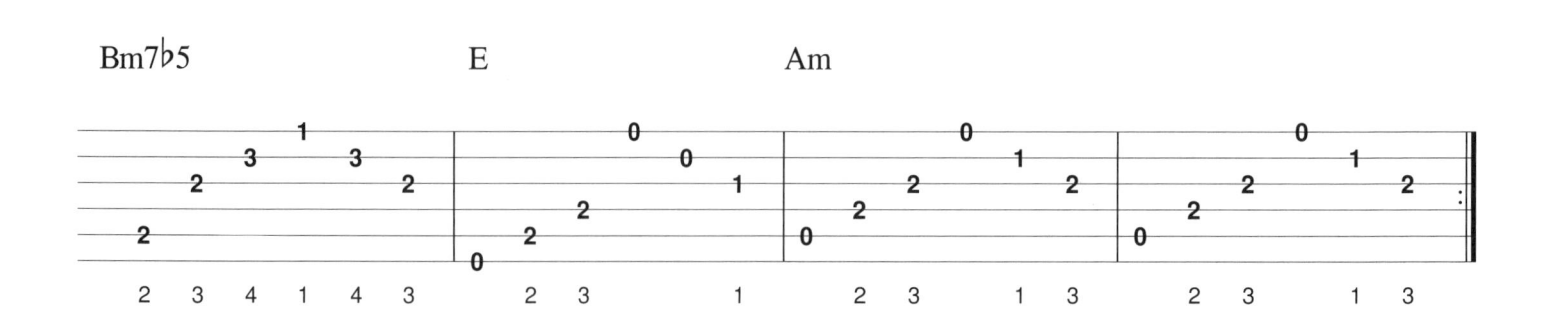

Natural Minor Scales

Many modern Rock and Blues players have incorporated the use of full natural minor scales into their soloing. The pentatonic scales you've already learned are abbreviated versions of the regular major and minor scales. The pentatonic scales contain five notes; the natural minor scale contains seven notes. The word "natural" refers to the fact that the scale is in its original unaltered state. The A natural minor scale is particularly unique because this key contains all natural notes (no sharp or flat notes). The notes in an A natural minor scale are A - B - C - D - E - F - G. The natural minor scale can be used to create more complex and interesting melodies.

Below are the first two positions of the A natural minor scale shown ascending and descending. The root notes have all been circled on the staff and scale diagrams. After you've memorized these two positions, log on to the Lesson Support Site to get the other three.

1st Position A Minor Scale

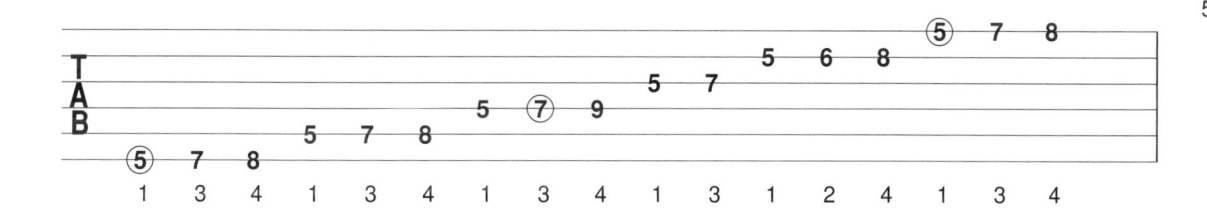

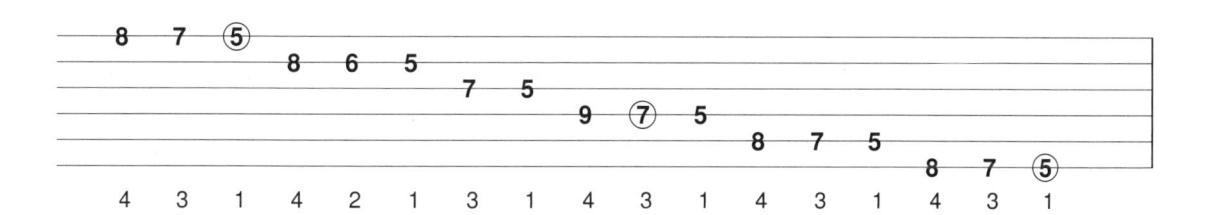

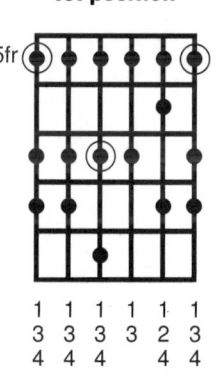

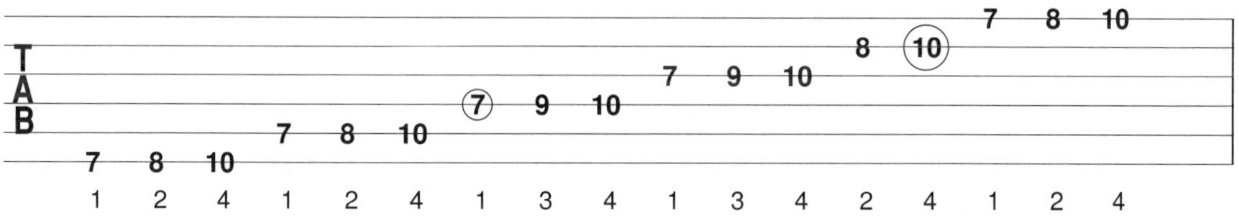

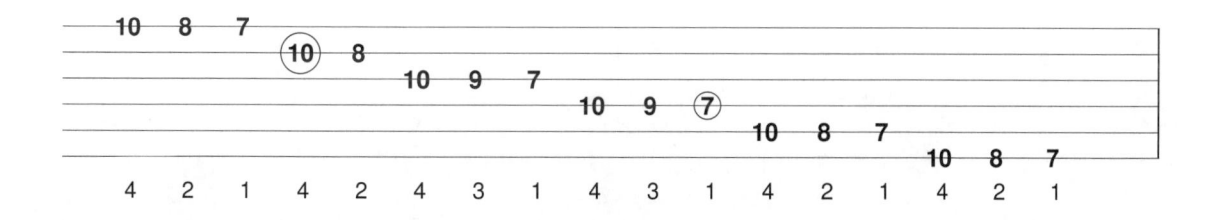

2nd Position A Minor Scale

81

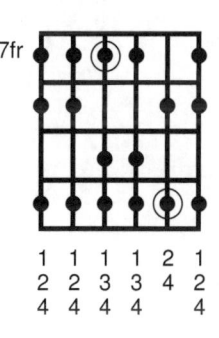

Melodic Lead

You can play leads over the previous modern blues progression using these scales. Here is an example lead that was improvised during this lesson on the DVD. Play through the tab to get some ideas, then try creating your own leads.

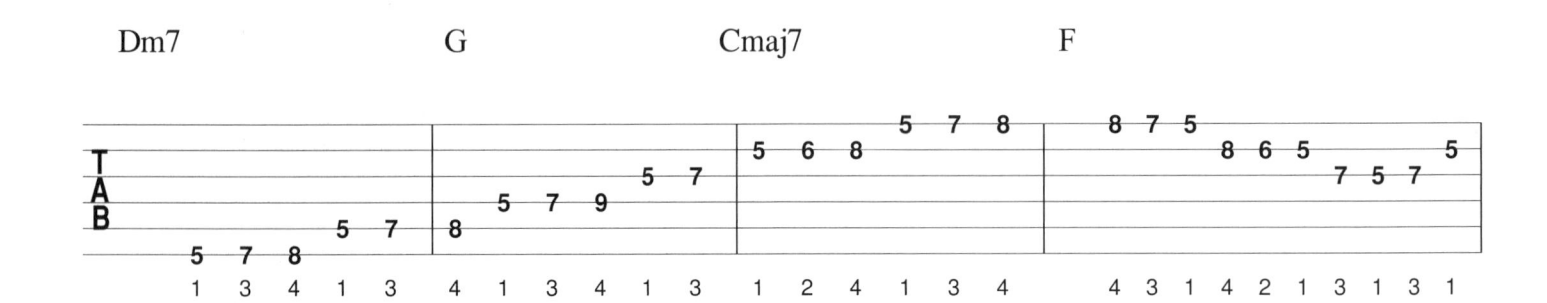

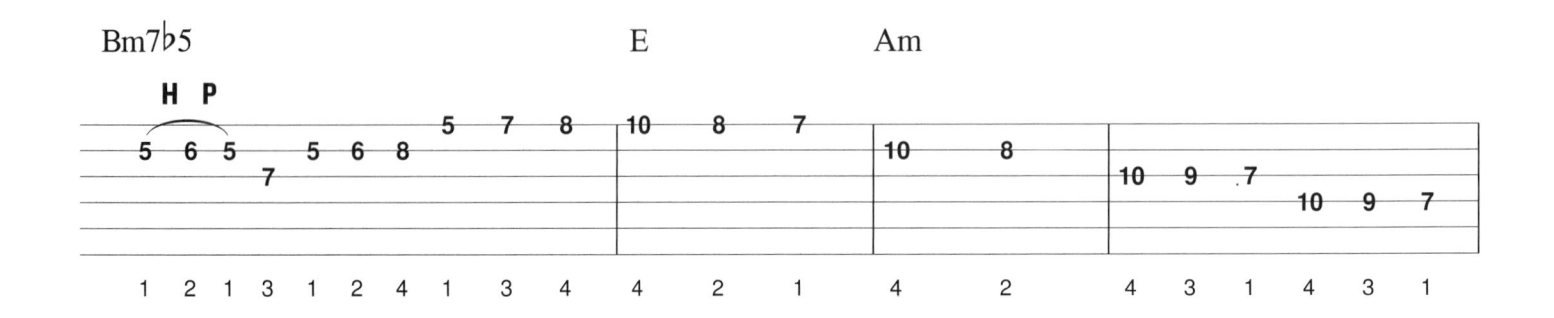

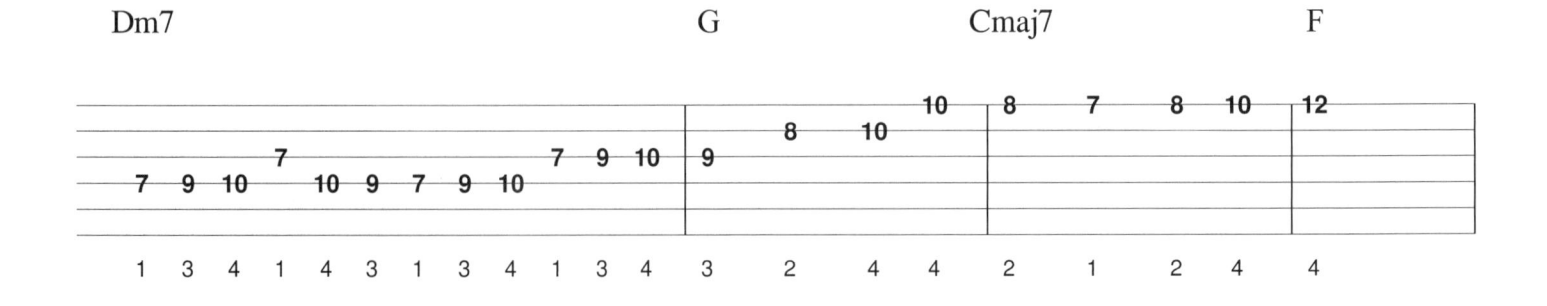

```
Dm7                    G                  Cmaj7                 F
                                                5  7  8       8  7  5
                                       5  6  8                      8  6  5             5
                              5  7                                           7  5  7
                     5  7  9
            5  7  8
  1  3  4   1  3  4   1  3  4   1  2  4   1  3  4   4  3  1  4  2  1  3  1  3  1
```

```
Bm7♭5                              E                  Am
  H  P
 ⌢
  5  6  5     5  6  8      5  7  8   10  8  7      10     8
            7                                                    10  9  7
                                                                        10  9  7
  1  2  1  3  1  2  4  1  3  4   4   2   1   4        2    4  3  1  4  3  1
```

```
Dm7                                G              Cmaj7                  F
                                              10  8  7  8  10  12
                                     8  10
              7              7  9  10   9
  7  9  10        10  9  7  9  10
  1  3  4  1  4  3  1  3  4  1  3  4   3    2    4    4    2    1    2    4    4
```

```
Bm7♭5                          E                      Am
                        H P  H P  H P
  13 12 10
        13 12 10       ⌢   ⌢   ⌢                              5  7  8
            12 10  9   9 10 9 7 9 7 5 7 5 4  5  4   7  5  4   4  5  7
                12 10 9                                 7  7  7
  4 3 1 4 3 1 4 2 1 4 2 1   1 2 1 1 3 1 1 3 1 1  2  1  2  2  1 2 2 2    1  1  4  1  1  2
```

82

Slide Technique and Rhythm

Slide guitar is a very popular technique used in blues. A slide is a cylinder worn on the ring finger of your fretting hand that allows you to slide notes and chords in a smooth, steady motion. Slides can be made of glass, metal, brass, or ceramic. You can even spontaneously use a shot glass or beer bottle as a slide.

In order to play pitches in tune with a slide, place the slide directly over the fret bar (not in between the frets). Use the frets as a visual reference point for where the notes will sound in tune. Touch the strings lightly with the slide; don't press down like you're fretting the note. Use the tip of the slide to play single notes or lay it flat to play chords. Open tunings work very well in conjunction with a slide because they allow you to slide full chords with one finger. Guitars that are set up to play with a slide usually have the *action* (string height) set a little higher than normal to keep the slide from hitting the frets.

A good way to begin to get the slide technique down is to play through the pentatonic scale using a slide. Try it in the 1st position, sliding from the first to the second notes along each string. Remember not to press down with the slide, just allow it to lightly touch the strings.

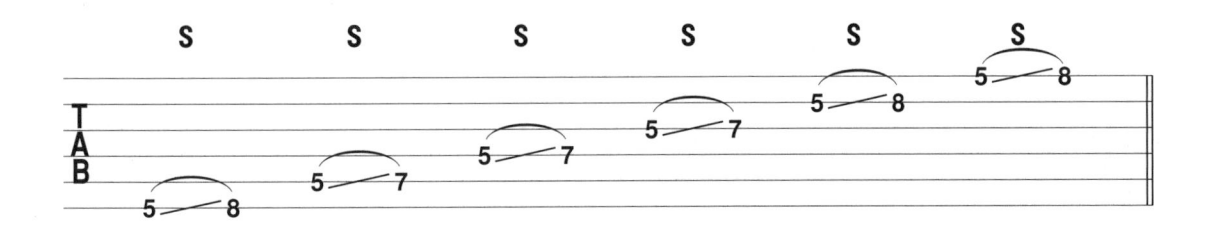

```
      S        S        S        S        S        S
                                                 5 — 8
                                        5 — 8
                               5 — 7
                      5 — 7
             5 — 7
   5 — 8
```

The following exercise is a typical blues rock rhythm played with a slide. This riff has been used to make up countless songs, so it should sound very familiar to you. The first measure (before the repeat sign) is called a *pickup*. It represents a partial measure of music that leads into the main repeated riff.

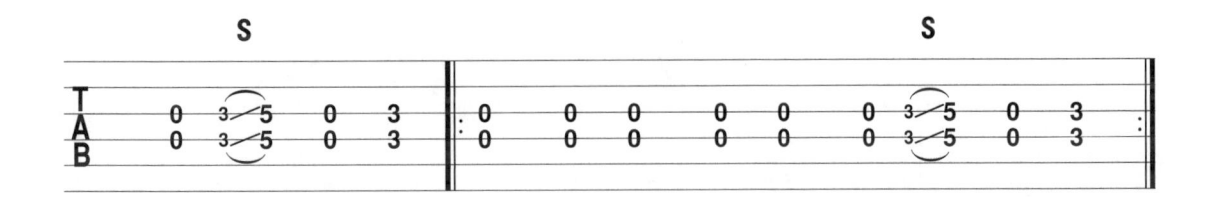

```
         S                                              S
   0  3—5   0   3  ||: 0    0   0    0   0   0  3—5   0   3 :||
   0  3—5   0   3  ||: 0    0   0    0   0   0  3—5   0   3 :||
```

83

E Blues Riff Rhythm

For the last section of this program, let's go over a single note riff rhythm in E. After you learn the rhythm, you can solo over the backing track using the E blues scales and all of the techniques we've covered. The progression is also based on a I - IV - V, 12-bar blues style; the chord names above the tab staff are there as a reference to outline the basic harmony.

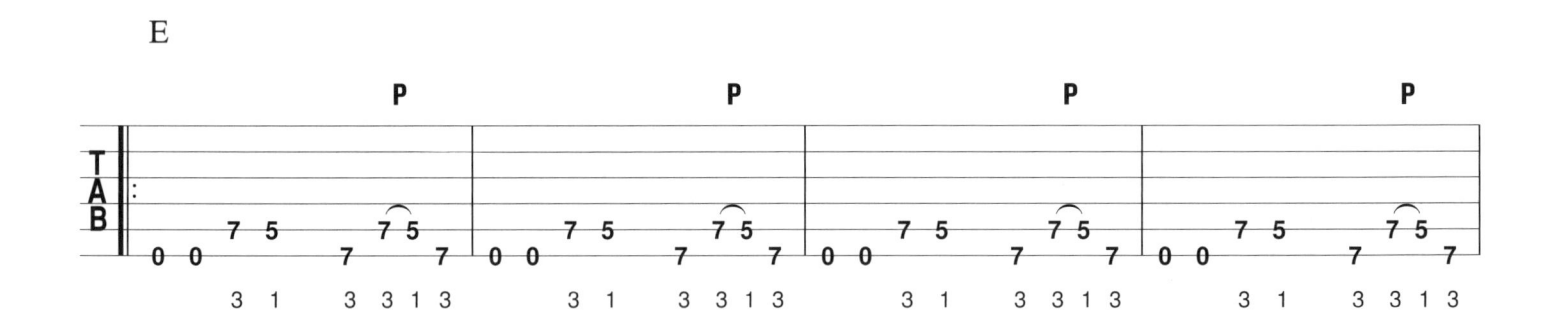

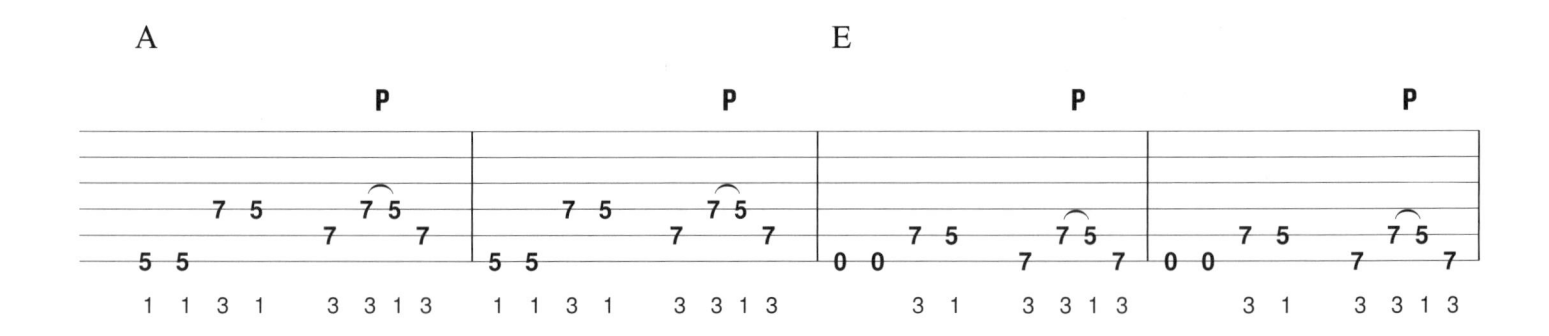

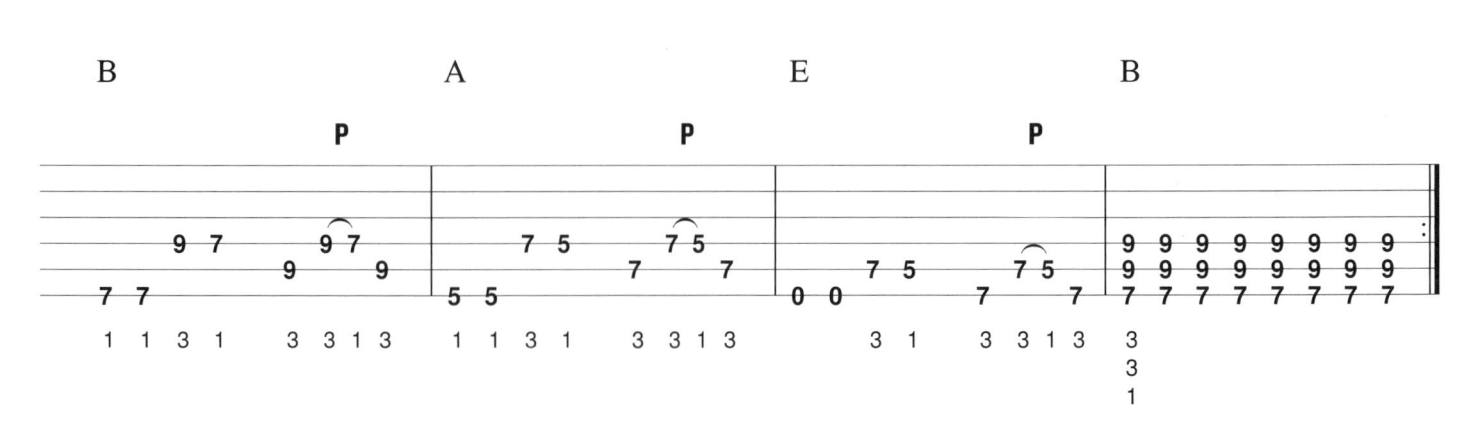

E Blues Solo

The following solo is the first part of the example lead on the DVD program. Try some of these riffs, then create your own and work on your improvisational skills using all of the techniques and styles you've learned. Log on to www.rockhousemethod.com and join our online community for additional information and resources.

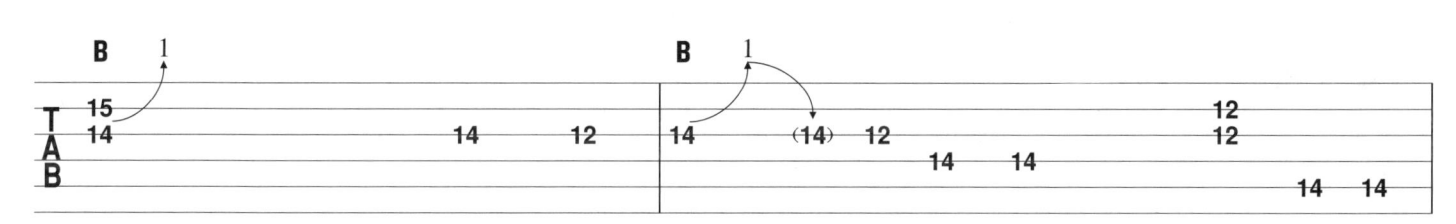

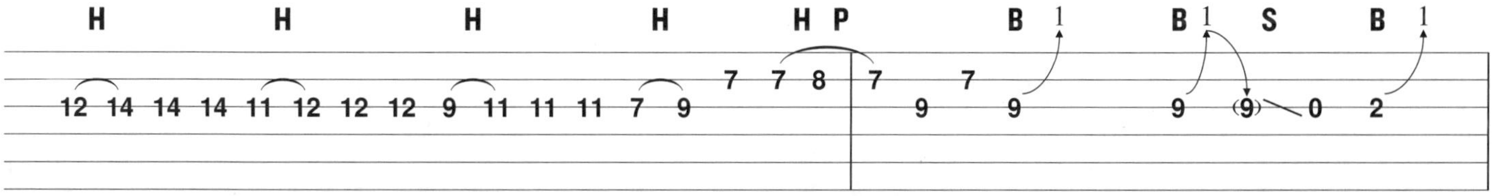

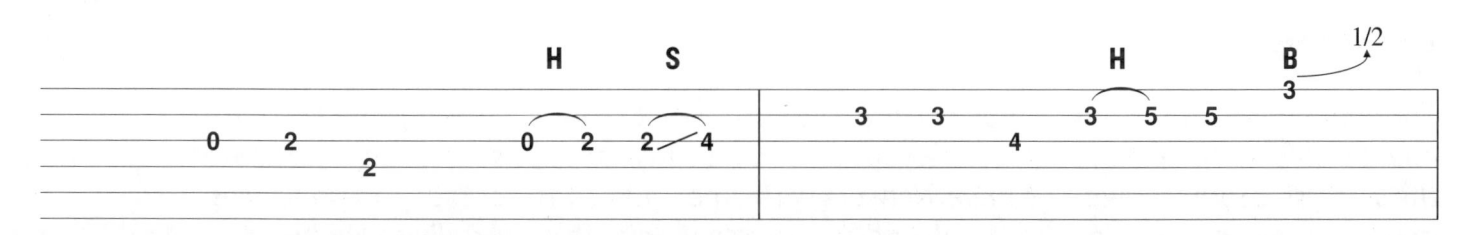

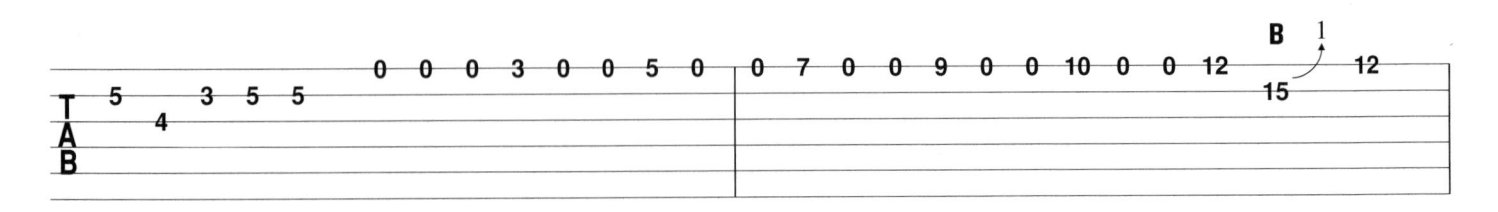

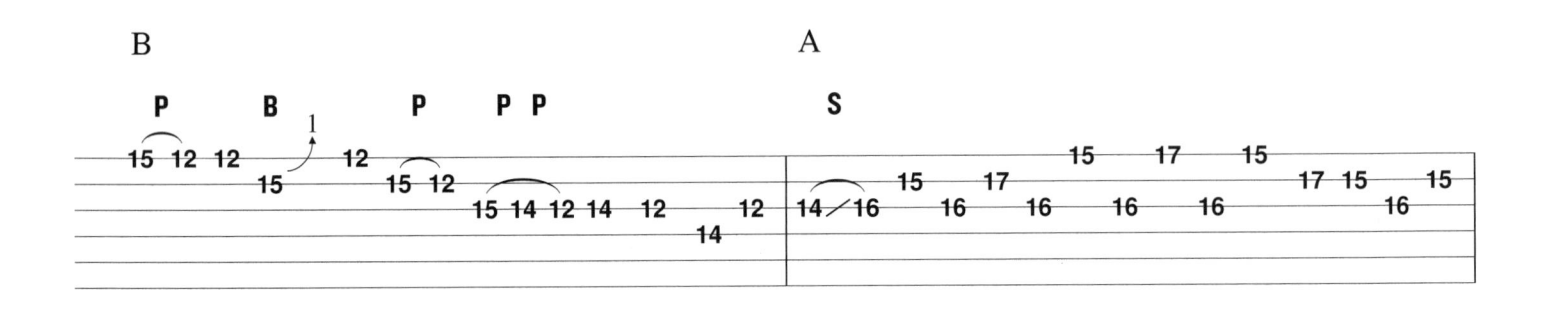

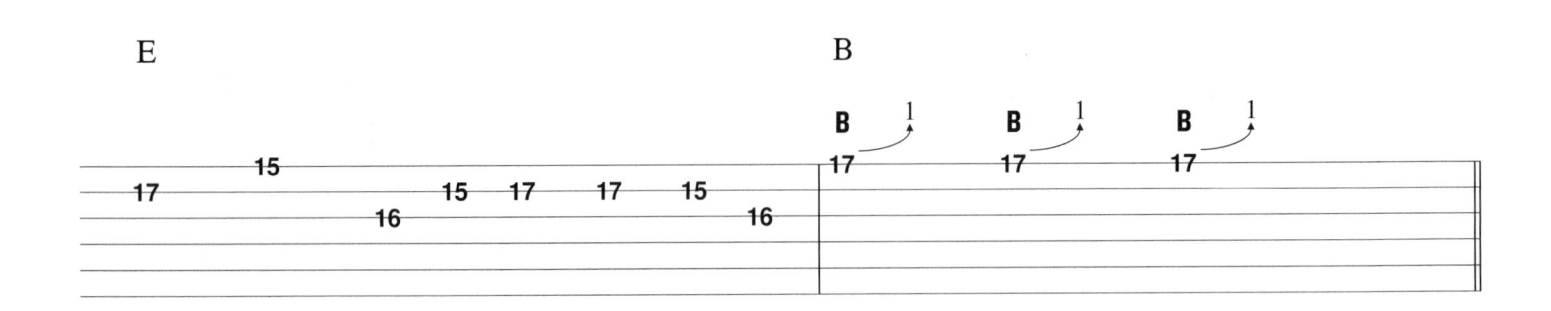

end of chapter 10

Congratulations! You've just completed all of the lessons on CD disc 2. By using your lifetime membership to the Lesson Support Site, you can continue to progress as a guitarist and utilize the limitless resources avialable there. Network with other musicians, post your original ideas and compositions and browse through additional lessons and tablature online. Download the many backing tracks available and jam along with the Rock House instructors!

Chord Glossary

Here is a collection of new chords for you to learn. Knowing many chords will give you a collection of music building blocks that you can use to learn your favorite songs or write your own masterpiece. Make sure to pick the notes separately first then start strumming away.

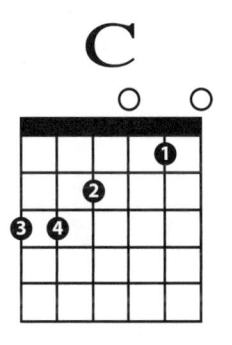

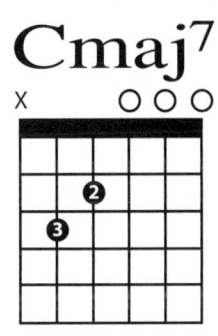

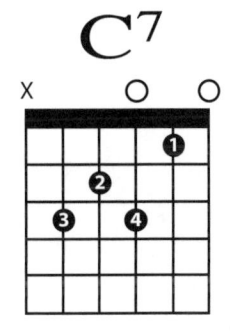

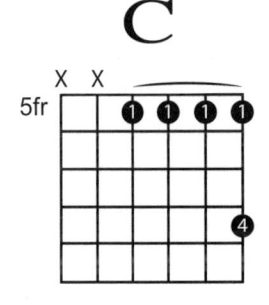

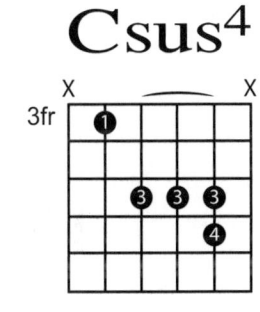

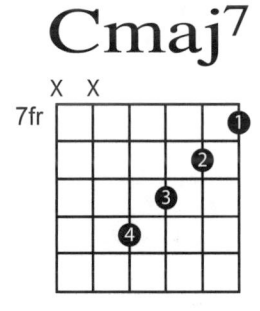

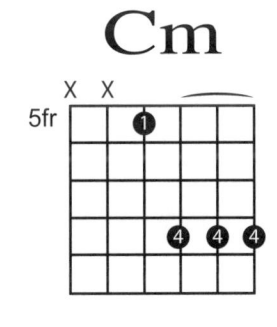

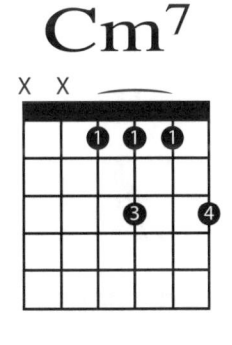

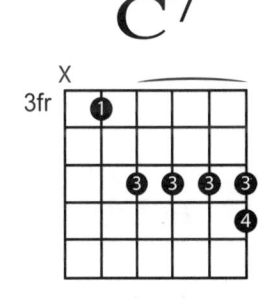

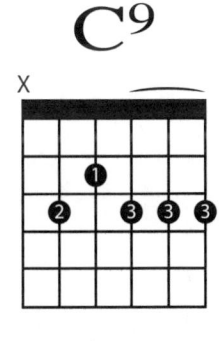

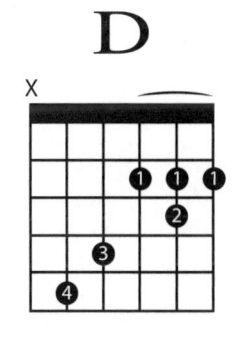

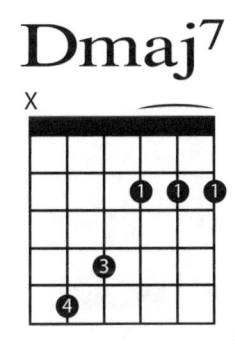

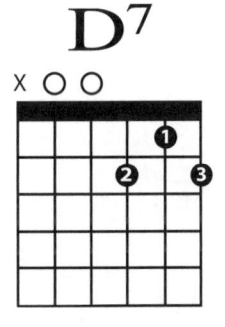

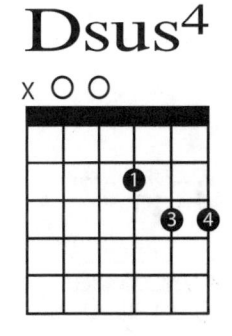

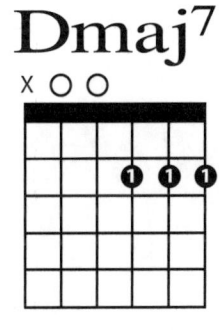

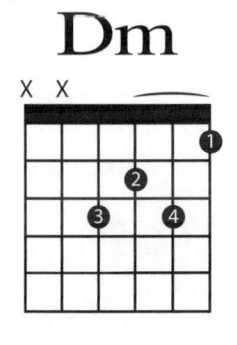

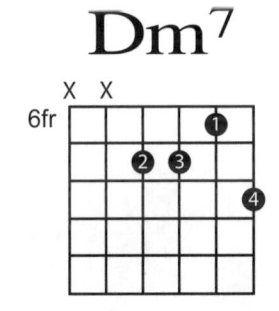

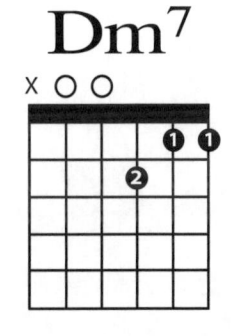

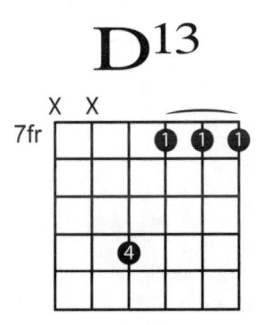

E Emaj⁷ E⁷ E⁹ Esus⁴

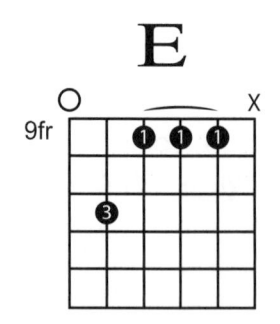

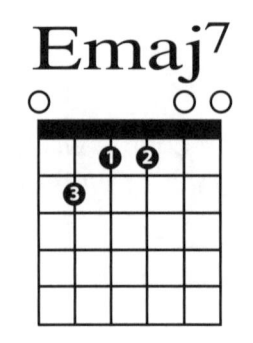

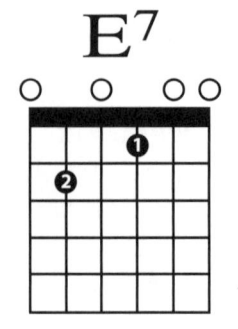

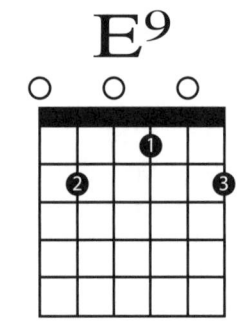

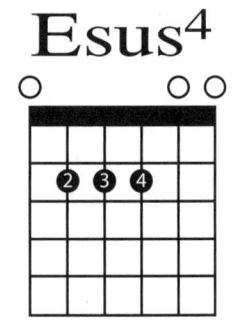

Esus² Em⁷ Em⁷ Em⁹

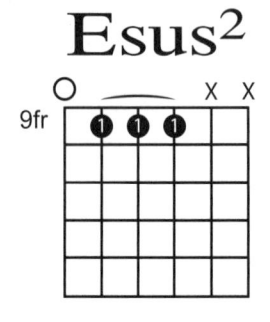

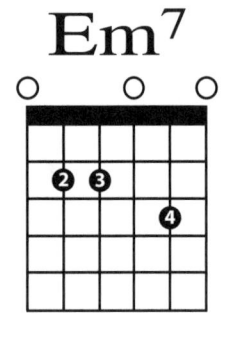

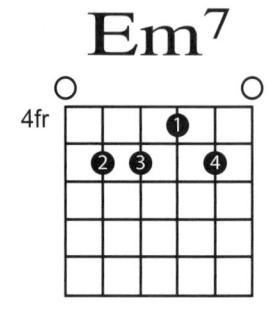

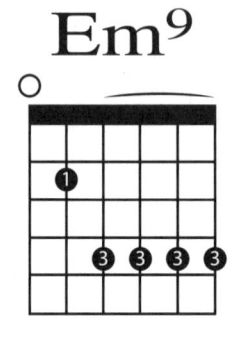

F Fmaj⁷ F⁷ Fm Fm⁷

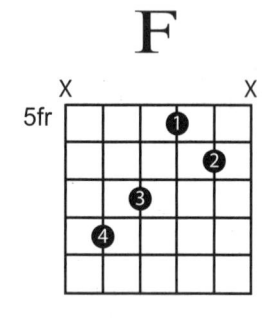

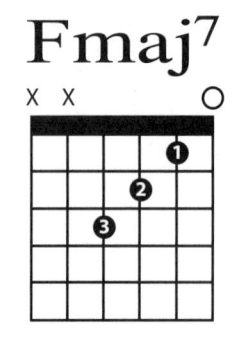

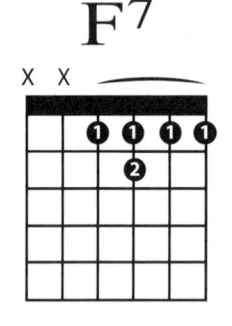

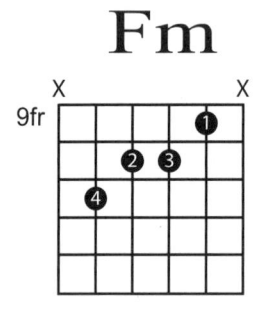

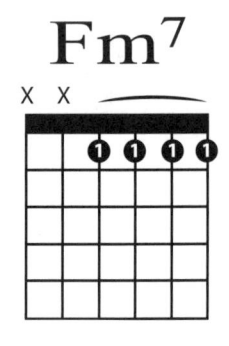

Fm⁷ Fsus⁴ Fm⁶

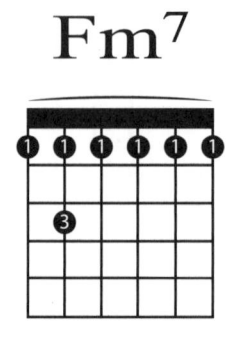

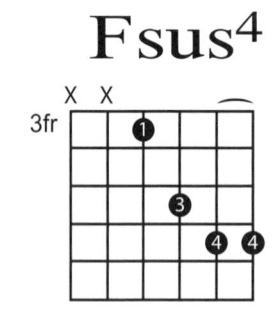

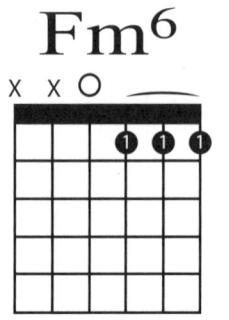

Gmaj^7

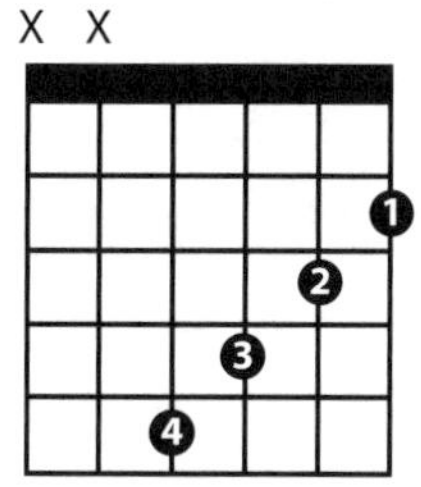

G^7

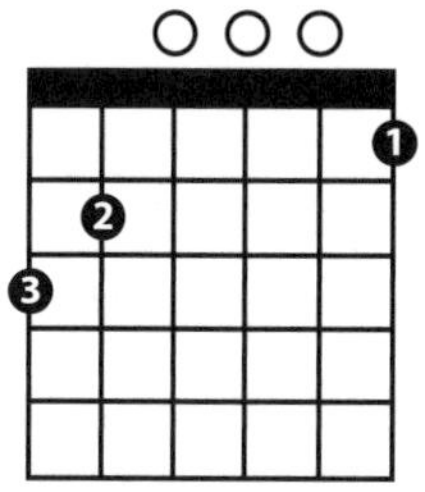

G^7

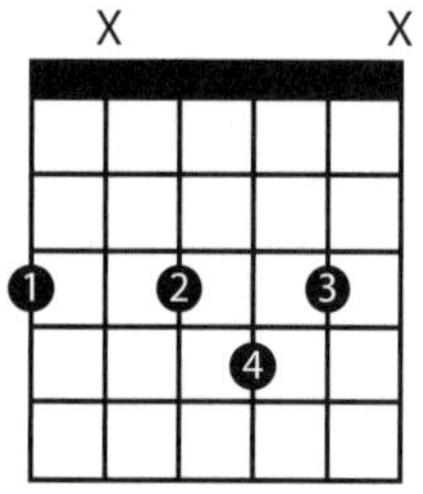

G^{7}sus^4

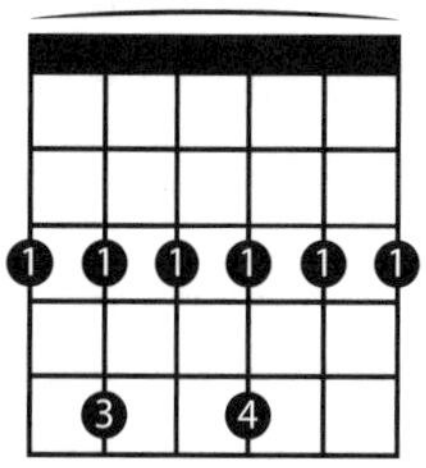

G^9

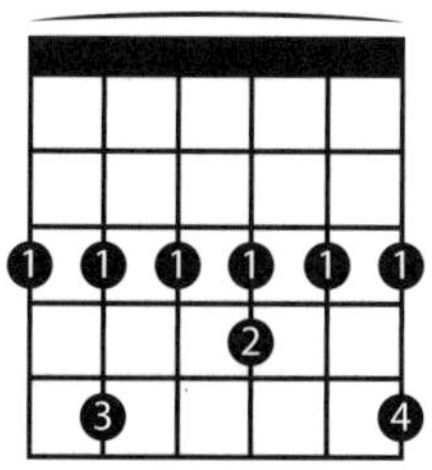

G^{13}

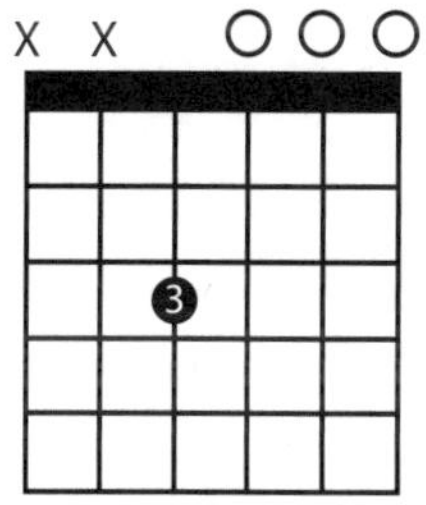

Gm^7

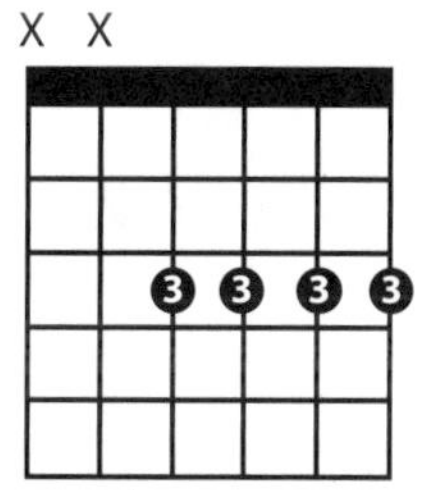

Gm

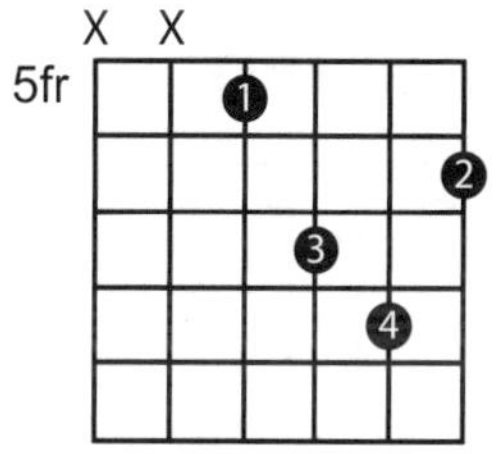

A^6

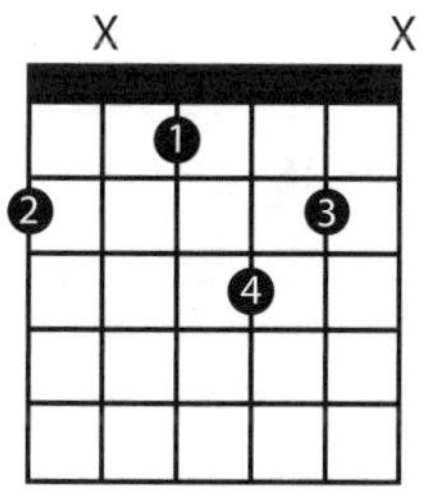

Amaj^7

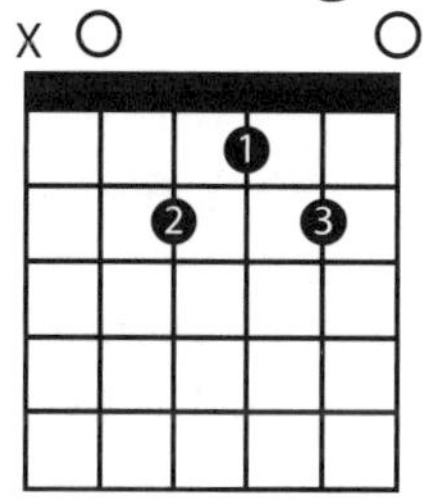

A^7

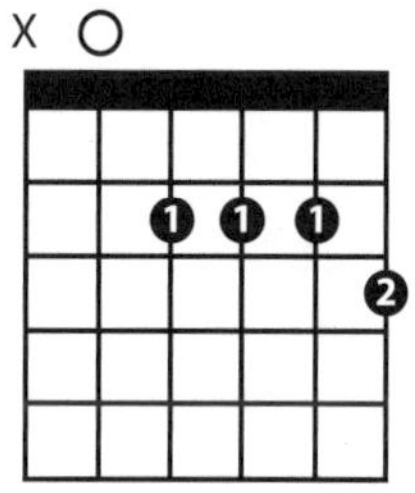

A^9

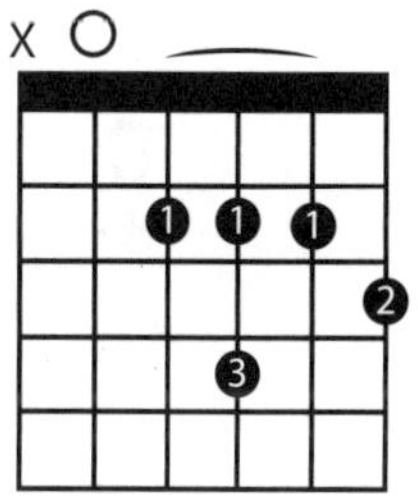

Am

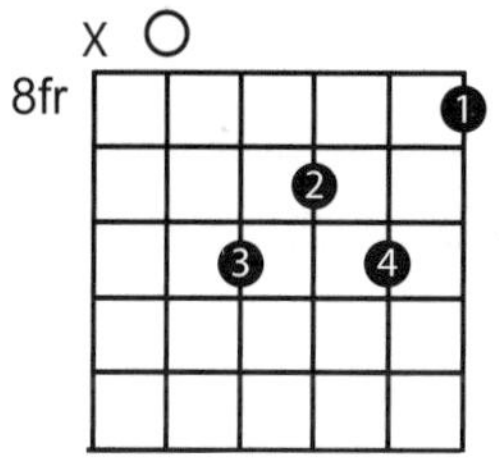

Am^7

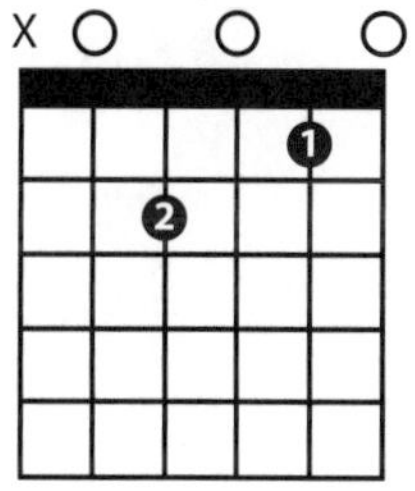

Am^6

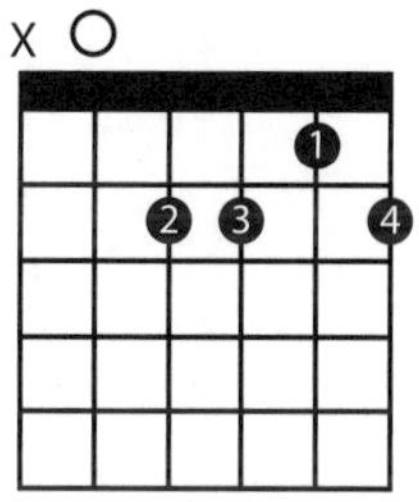

Asus^4

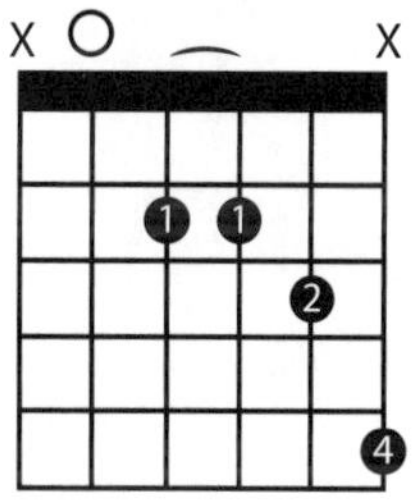

Bmaj⁷ B⁷ B⁹ B⁷♯⁹ B¹³

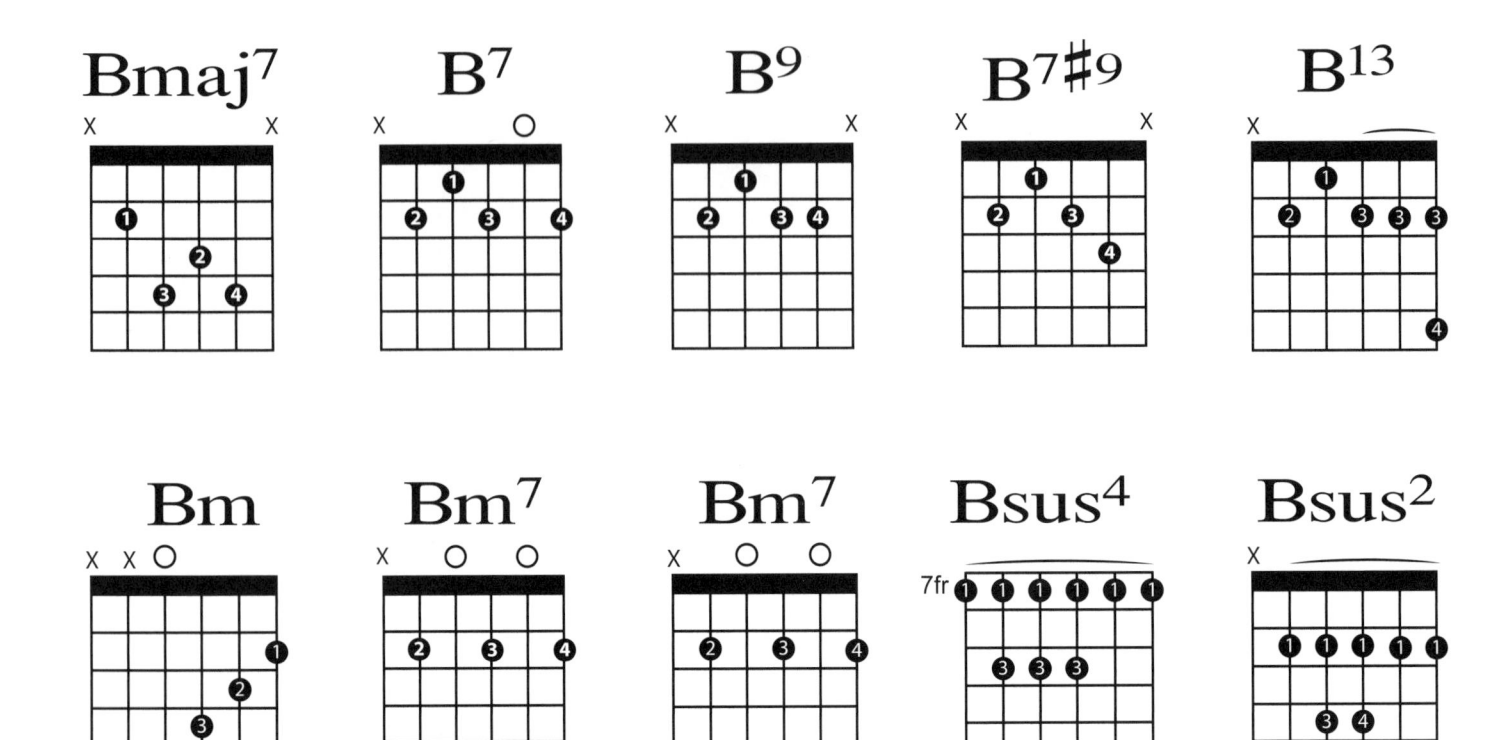

Bm Bm⁷ Bm⁷ Bsus⁴ Bsus²

Circle of 4th's and 5th's

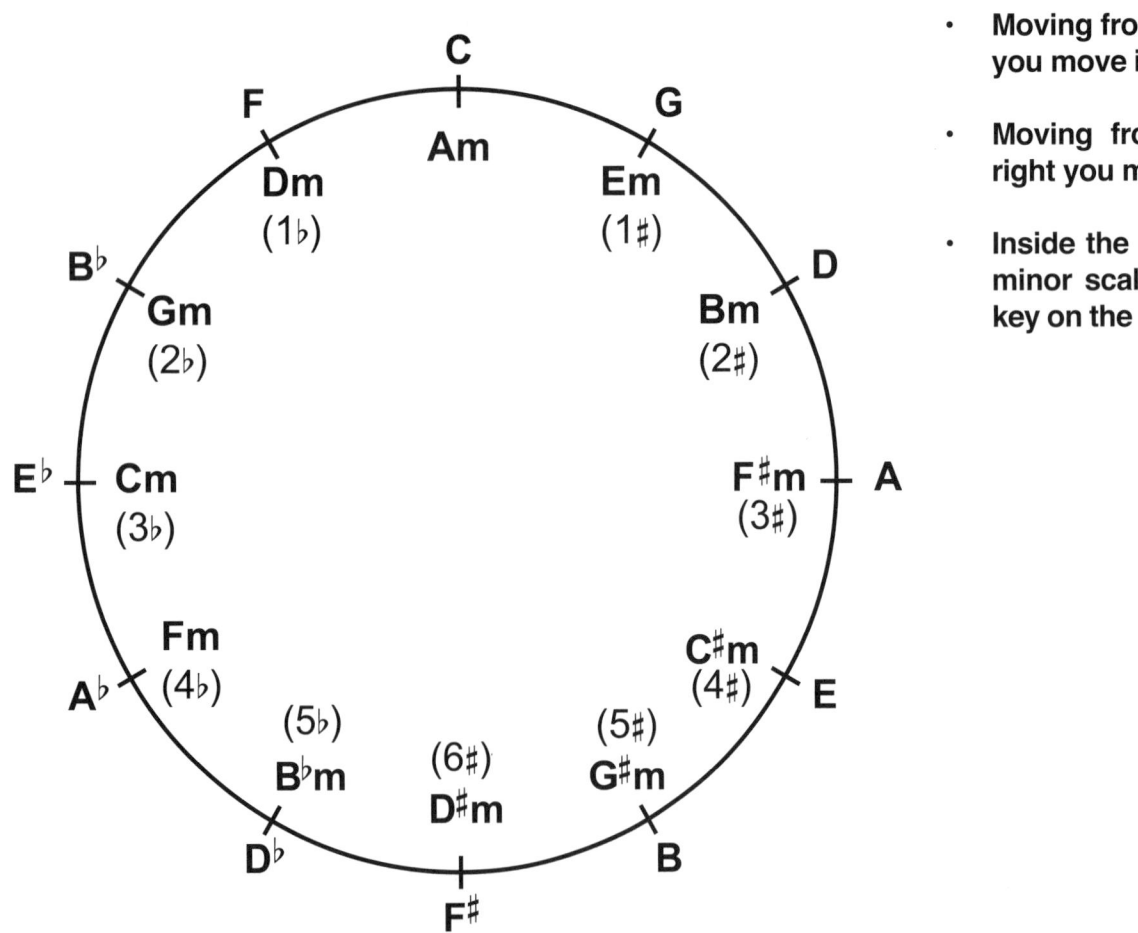

- Moving from C Major to the left you move in fourths.

- Moving from C Major to the right you move in fifths.

- Inside the circle is the relative minor scale for each adjacent key on the outside of the circle.

90

All Keys Relative Minor

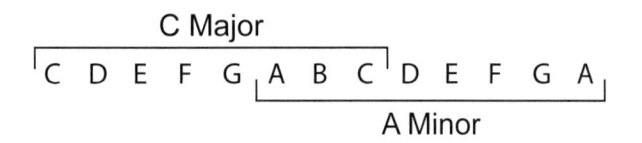

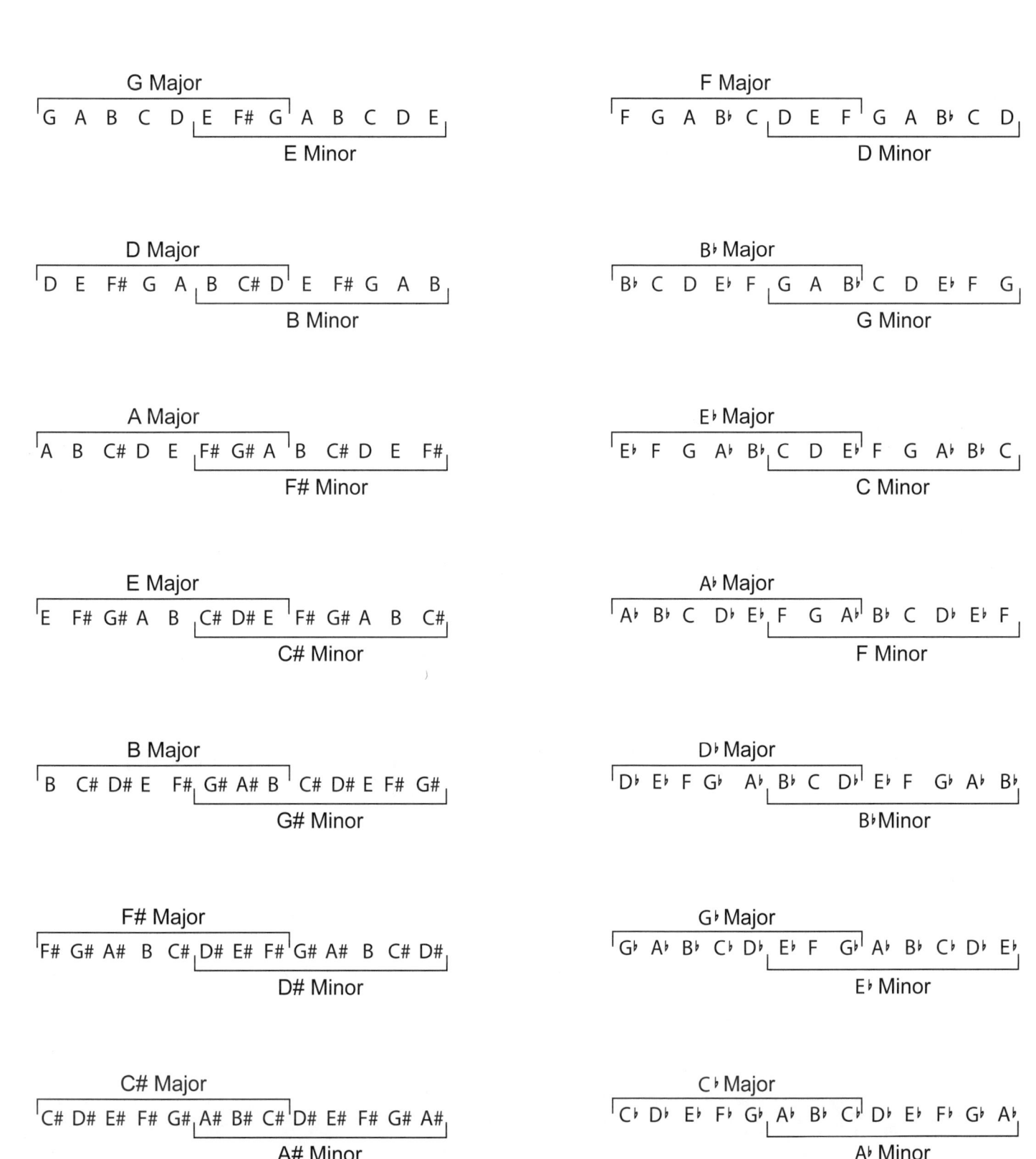

C Major
C D E F G A B C D E F G A
A Minor

G Major
G A B C D E F# G A B C D E
E Minor

F Major
F G A B♭ C D E F G A B♭ C D
D Minor

D Major
D E F# G A B C# D E F# G A B
B Minor

B♭ Major
B♭ C D E♭ F G A B♭ C D E♭ F G
G Minor

A Major
A B C# D E F# G# A B C# D E F#
F# Minor

E♭ Major
E♭ F G A♭ B♭ C D E♭ F G A♭ B♭ C
C Minor

E Major
E F# G# A B C# D# E F# G# A B C#
C# Minor

A♭ Major
A♭ B♭ C D♭ E♭ F G A♭ B♭ C D♭ E♭ F
F Minor

B Major
B C# D# E F# G# A# B C# D# E F# G#
G# Minor

D♭ Major
D♭ E♭ F G♭ A♭ B♭ C D♭ E♭ F G♭ A♭ B♭
B♭ Minor

F# Major
F# G# A# B C# D# E# F# G# A# B C# D#
D# Minor

G♭ Major
G♭ A♭ B♭ C♭ D♭ E♭ F G♭ A♭ B♭ C♭ D♭ E♭
E♭ Minor

C# Major
C# D# E# F# G# A# B# C# D# E# F# G# A#
A# Minor

C♭ Major
C♭ D♭ E♭ F♭ G♭ A♭ B♭ C♭ D♭ E♭ F♭ G♭ A♭
A♭ Minor

Full Major Scales

A Major

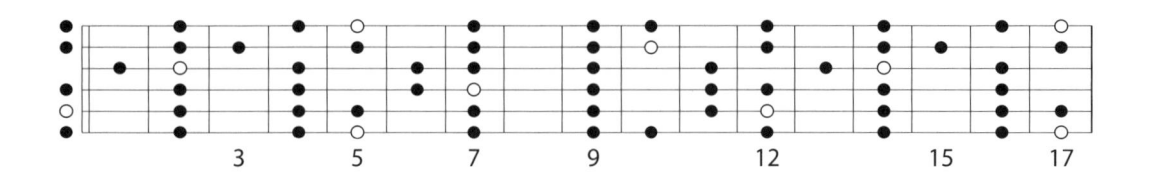

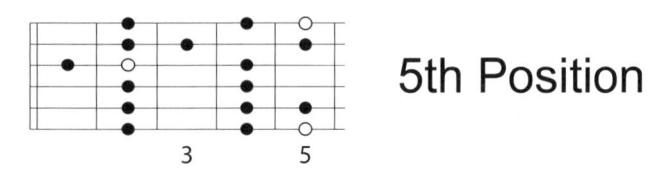

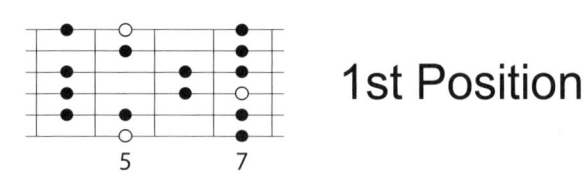

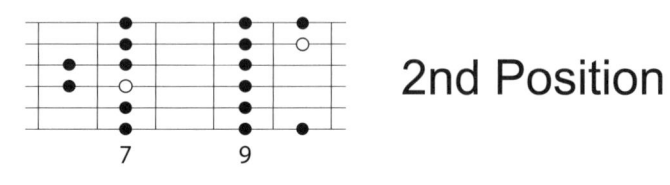

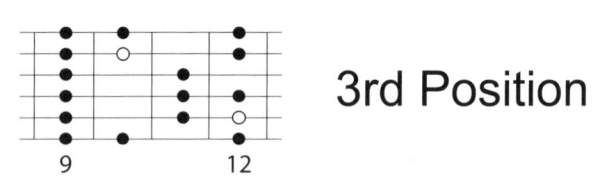

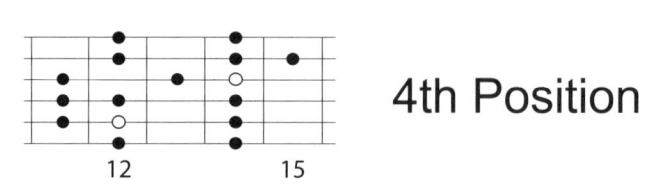

5th Position

1st Position

2nd Position

3rd Position

4th Position

Major Pentatonic Scales

A Major

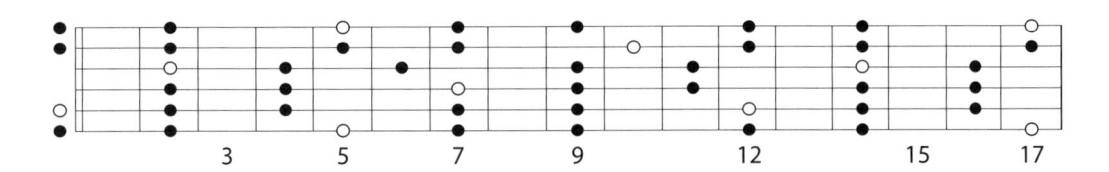

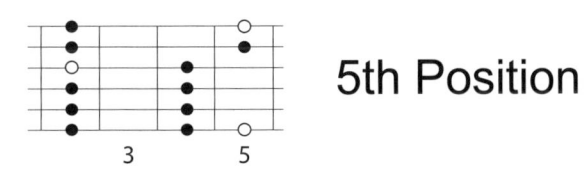

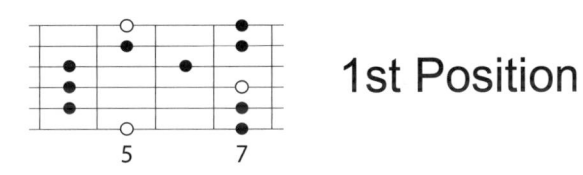

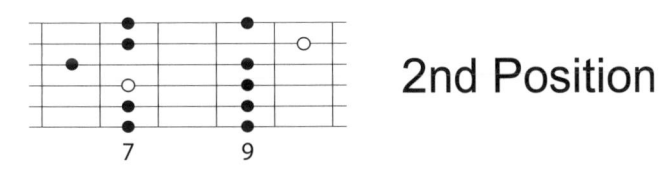

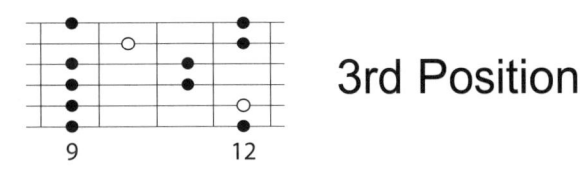

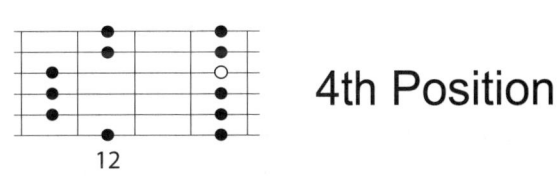

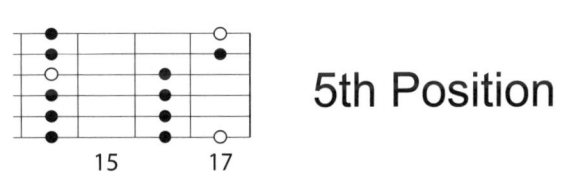

5th Position

1st Position

2nd Position

3rd Position

4th Position

5th Position

Three Note Per String Minor Scales
A Minor

5th Position

6th Position

7th Position

1st Position

2nd Position — 2nd Position

3rd Position — 3rd Position

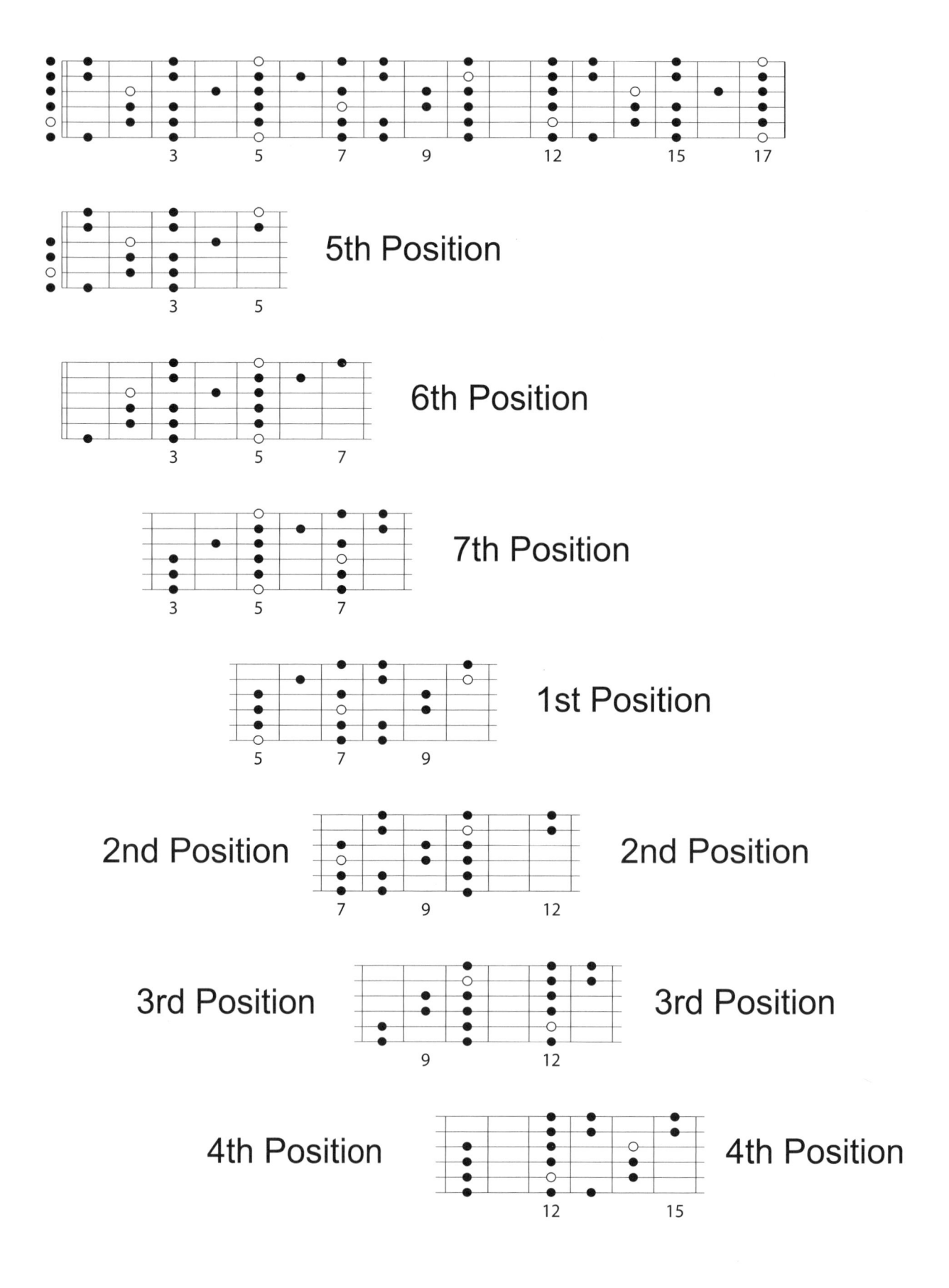

4th Position — 4th Position

Minor Pentatonic Scales
A Minor

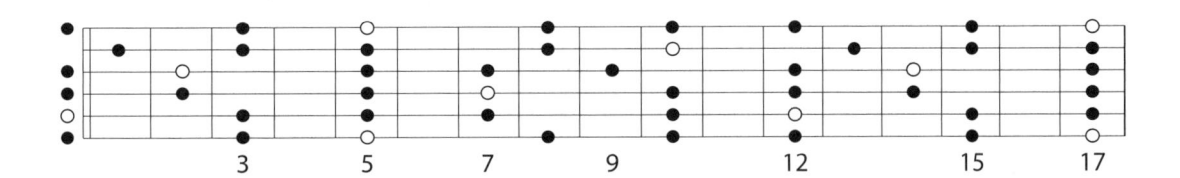

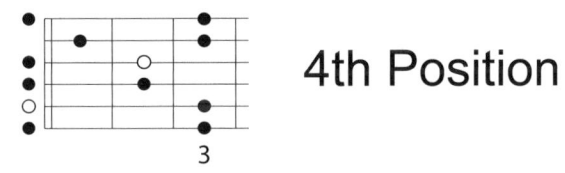

4th Position

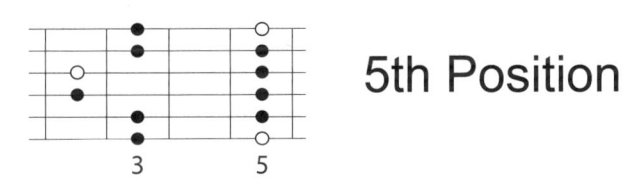

5th Position

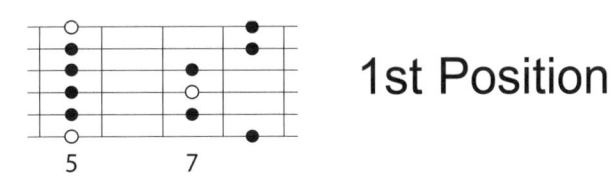

1st Position

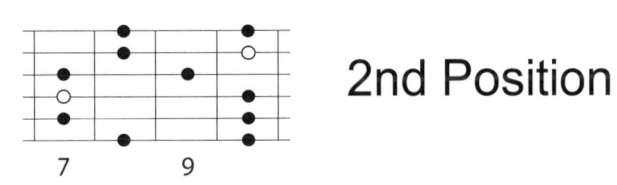

2nd Position

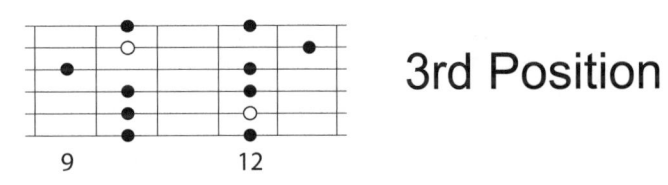

3rd Position

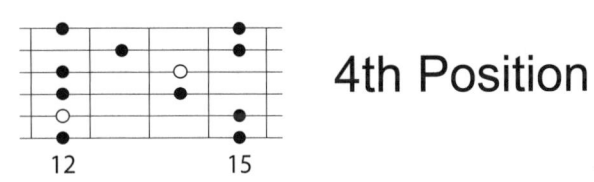

4th Position

NEVER COMING BACK

Here's the first part of the blues extravaganza "Never Coming Back" from my CD, **Drive**. The song starts out with two separate guitars trading riffs, then coming together in perfect harmony. The audio for this section is available on the included CD. You can also download this track as well as other songs from Drive at www.rockhousemethod.com.

- John McCarthy

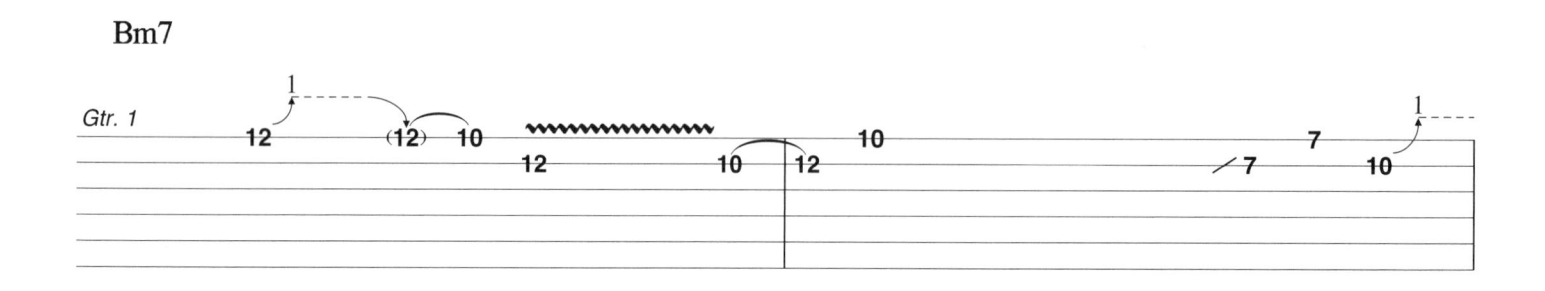

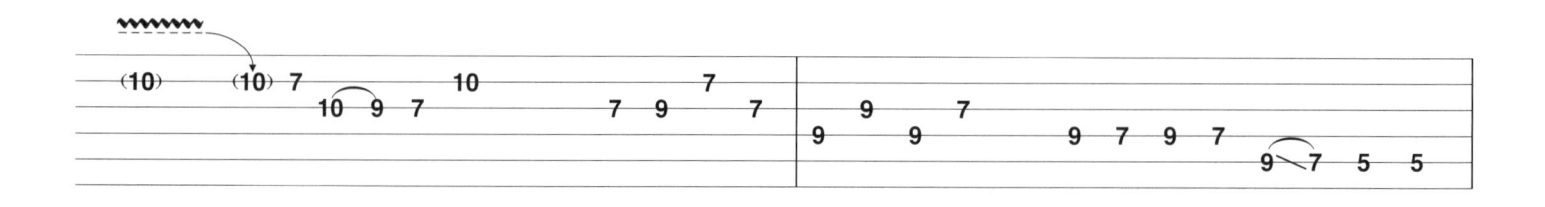

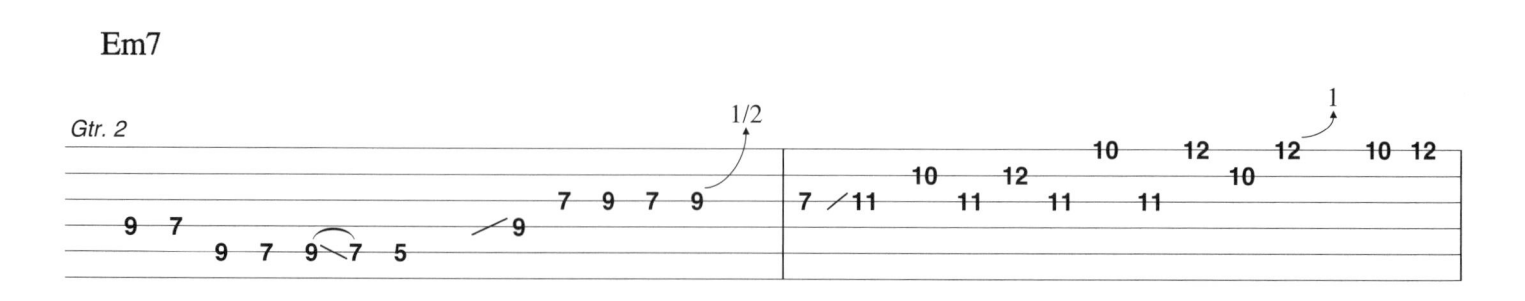

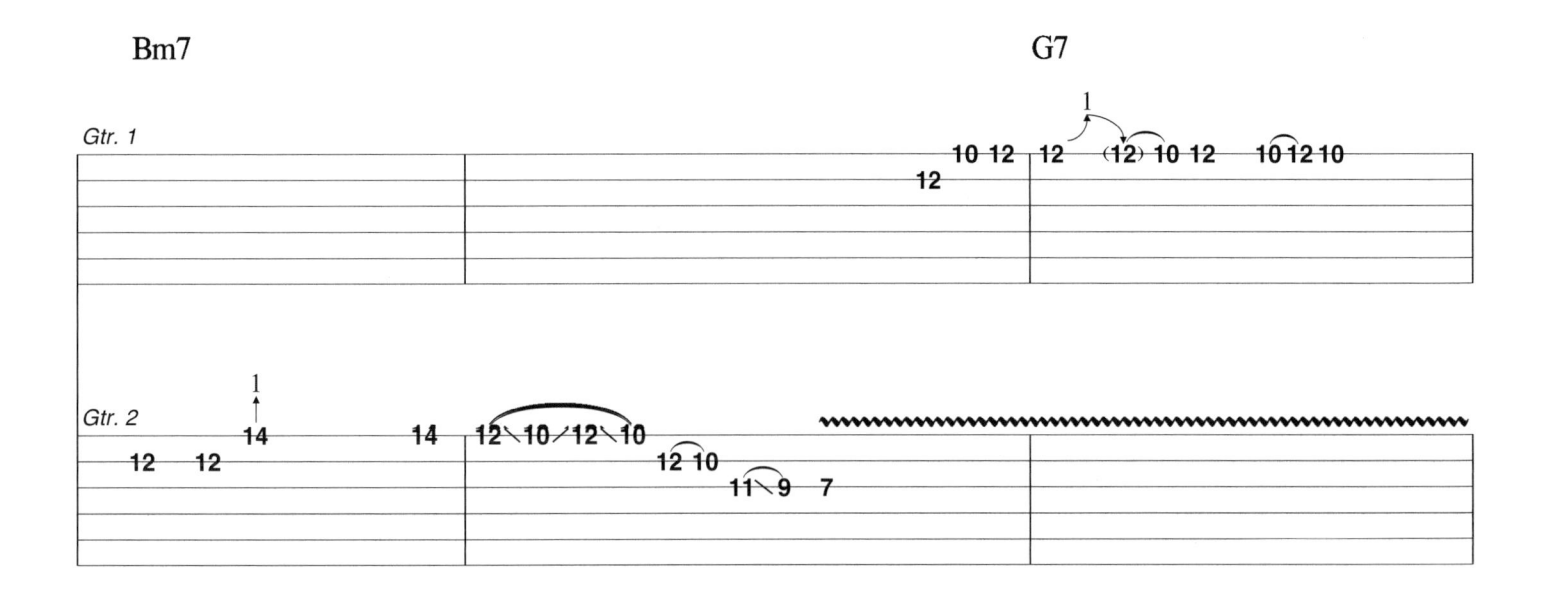

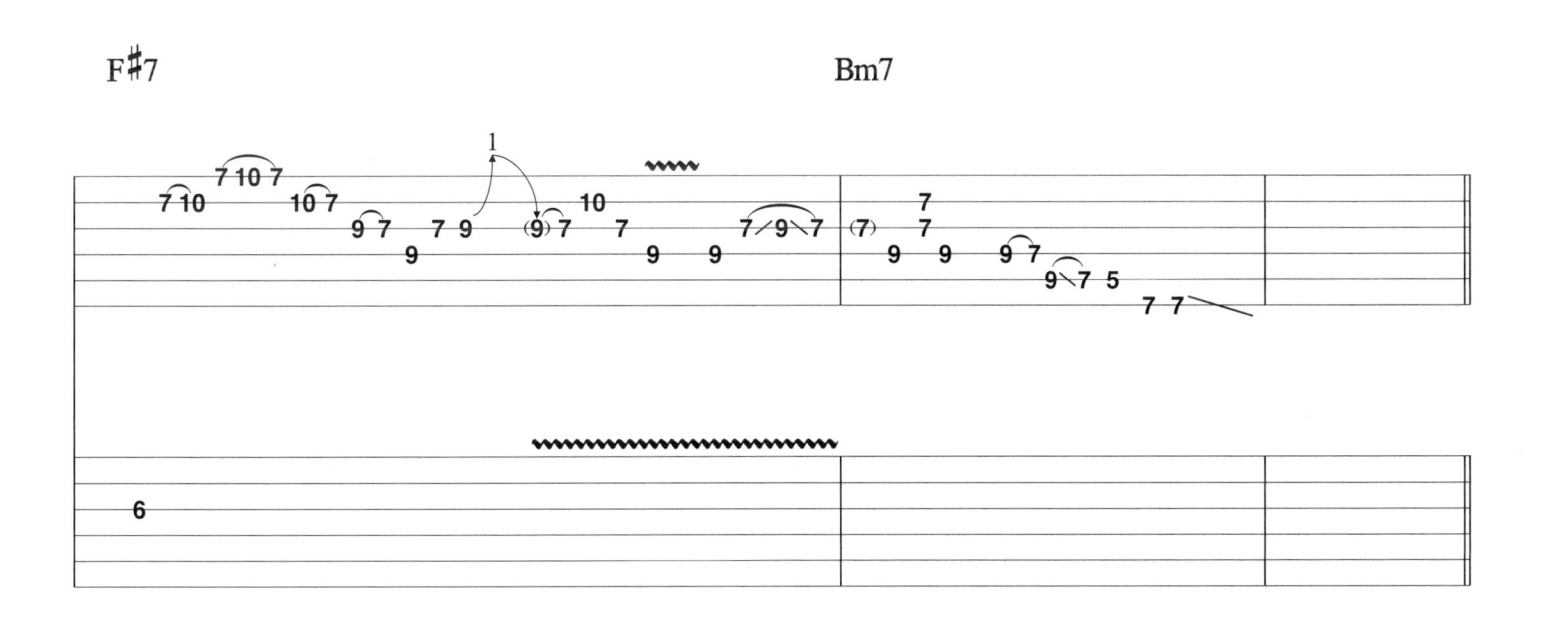

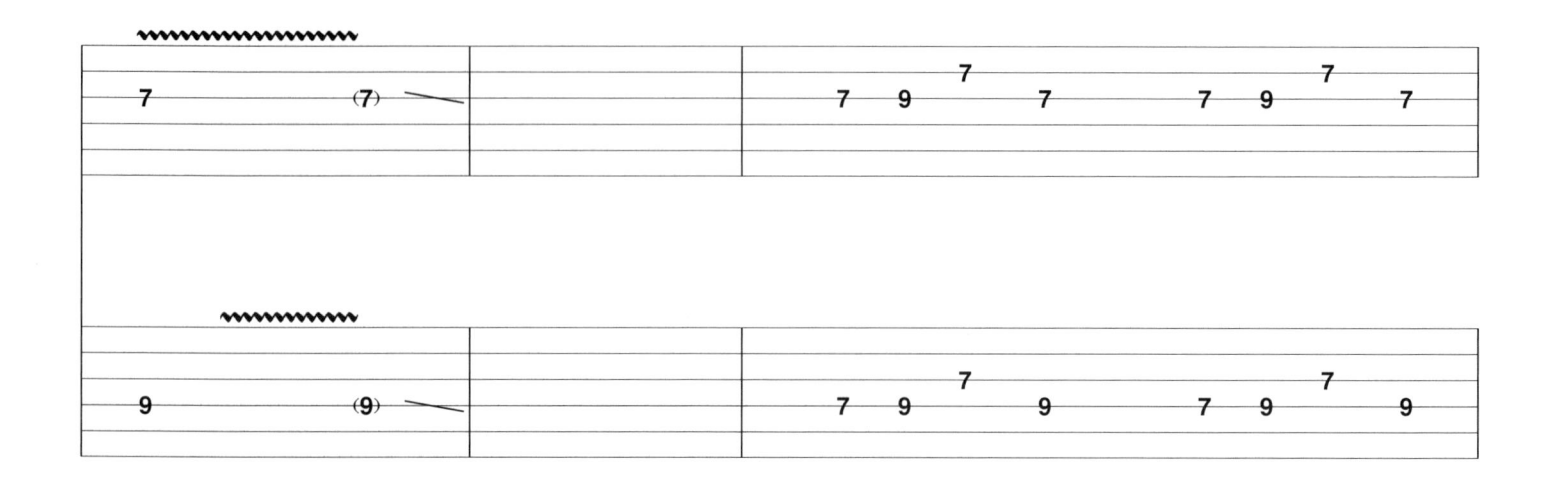

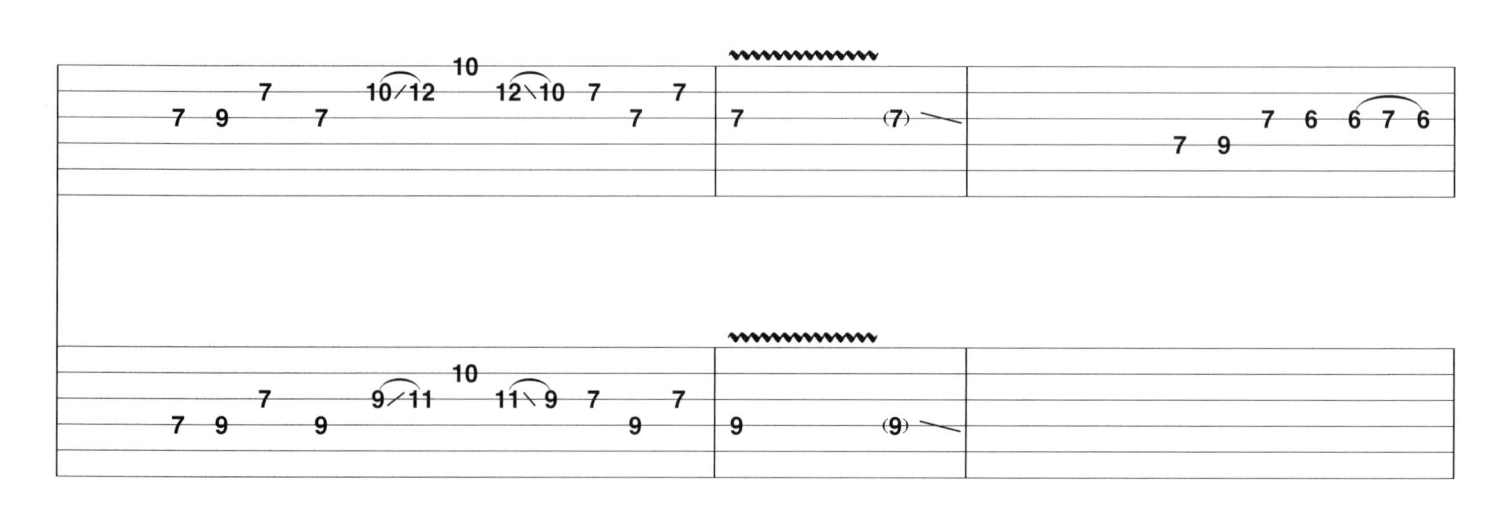

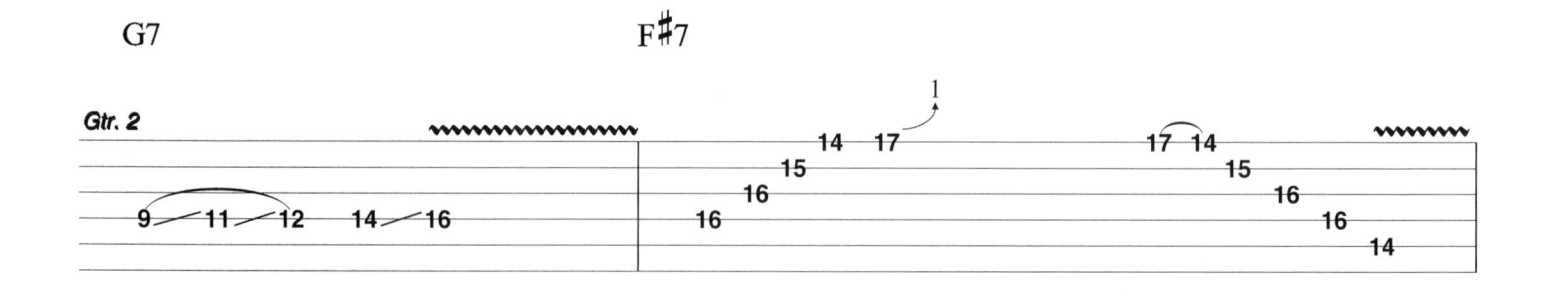

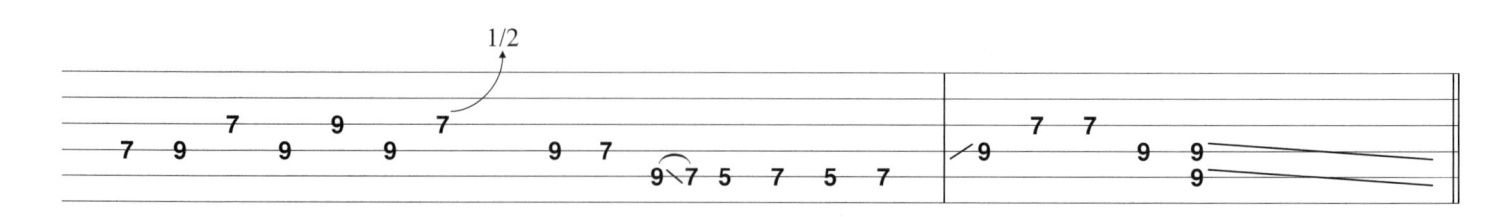

Changing a String

Old guitar strings may break or lose their tone and become harder to keep in tune. You might feel comfortable at first having a teacher or someone at a music store change your strings for you, but eventually you will need to know how to do it yourself. Changing the strings on a guitar is not as difficult as it may seem and the best way to learn how to do this is by practicing. Guitar strings are fairly inexpensive and you may have to go through a few to get it right the first time you try to restring your guitar. How often you change your strings depends entirely on how much you play your guitar, but if the same strings have been on it for months, it's probably time for a new set.

Most strings attach at the headstock in the same way, however electric and acoustic guitars vary in the way in which the string is attached at the bridge. Before removing the old string from the guitar, examine the way it is attached to the guitar and try to duplicate that with the new string. Acoustic guitars may use removeable bridge pins that fasten the end of the string to the guitar by pushing it into the bridge and securing it there. On some electric guitars, the string may need to be threaded through a hole in the back of the body.

Follow the series of photos below for a basic description of how to change a string. Before trying it yourself, read through the quick tips for beginners on the following page.

Use a string winder to loosen the string.

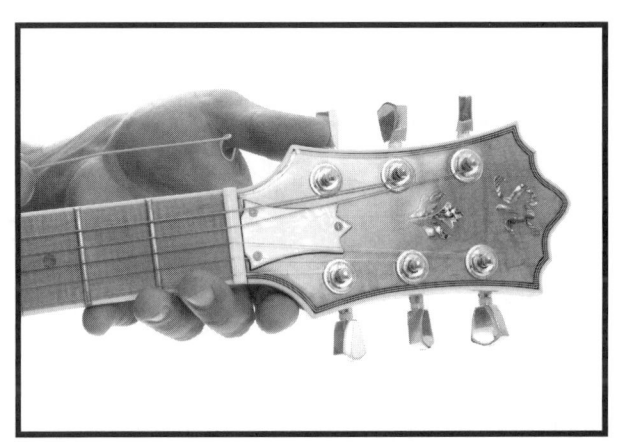

Remove the old string from the tuning post.

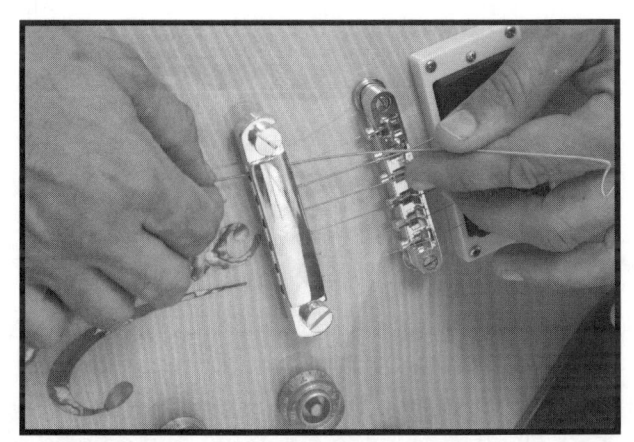

Pull the old string through the bridge and discard it.

Remove the new string from the packaging and uncoil it.

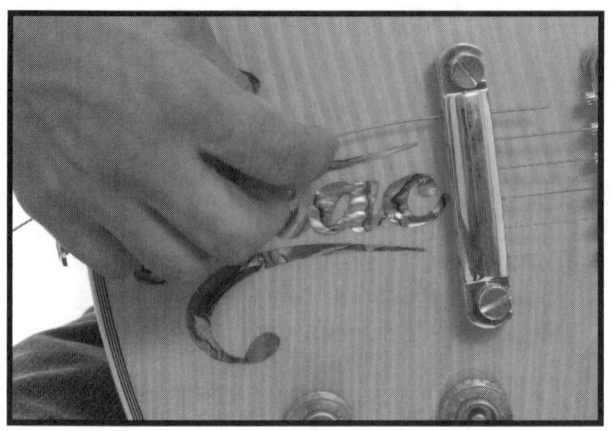

Thread the end of the new string through the bridge.

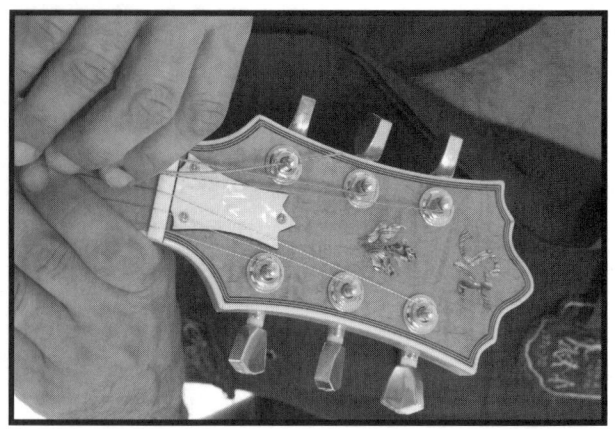

Pull the string along the neck and thread it through the small hole on the tuning post.

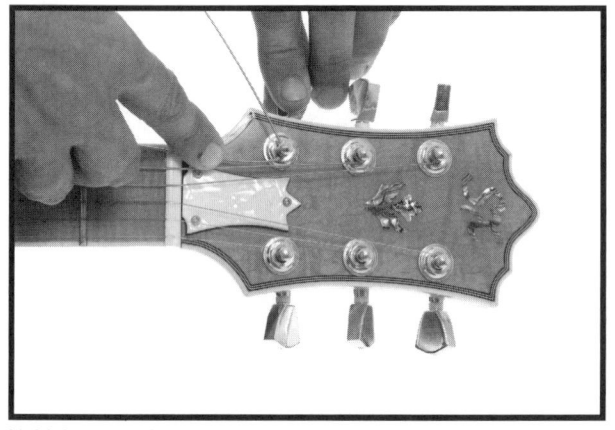

Hold the string in place just after the nut with your finger and tighten up the slack in the string with the machine head.

Carefully tighten the string and tune it to the proper pitch.

You can cut the old string off the guitar but you may want to unwind it instead and save it as a spare in case you break a string later.

Check to make sure you have the correct string in your hand before putting it on the guitar. The strings may be color coded at the end to help you identify them.

Be sure to wind the string around the tuning post in the proper direction (see photos), and leave enough slack to wind the string around the post several times. The string should wind around the post underneath itself to form a nice, neat coil.

Once the extra slack is taken up and the string is taught, tune it very gradually to pitch, being careful not to overtighten and accidentally break the new string.

Once the string is on the guitar and tightened up, you can cut the excess string sticking out from the tuning post with a wire cutter. The sharp tail end that is left can be bent downward with the wire cutter to get it out of the way and avoid cutting or stabbing your finger on it.

Check the ends of the string to make sure it is sitting correctly on the proper saddle and space on the nut.

New strings will go out of tune very quickly until they are broken in. You can gently massage the new string with your thumbs and fingers once it's on the guitar, slightly stretching the string out and helping to break it in. Then retune the string and repeat this process a few times for each string.

our roots

House of Blues is a home for live music and southern-inspired cuisine in an environment celebrating the African American cultural contributions to blues music and folk art. In 1992, our company converted an historical house in Cambridge, Massachusetts into the original House of Blues®. The original House of Blues opened its doors on Thanksgiving Day, 1992 feeding the homeless before opening to the public. Our commitment to serving the community will always be a priority.

We now have the pleasure of bringing live music to 16 major markets in the U. S. and Canada through our 10 club and 19 arena and amphitheatre venues. Come share the House of Blues experience. Get intimate with your favorite band in our Music Hall or enjoy soulful sounds and eats at our popular weekend Gospel Brunch. Savor down home, southern inspired cooking in the restaurant. Be a VIP for an exclusive night out in the membership club Foundation Room. Celebrate an important event in one of our cool private party rooms and take home a special souvenir from our retail store. We look forward to welcoming you to our house!

our mission

To create a profitable, principled global entertainment company.
To celebrate the diversity and brotherhood of world culture.
To promote racial and spiritual harmony through love, peace, truth, righteousness and non-violence.

musical diversity

In our Music Halls, you will find almost every music genre imaginable. Rock n' Roll, Punk, Alternative, Heavy Metal, Rap, Country, Hip-Hop, Rhythm and Blues, Rock en Español, Jazz, Zydeco, Folk, Electronica and many other genres grace our stages. We welcome and celebrate music as a form of art and expression.

Music is a celebration. We design and manage venues with the complete experience in mind. *Best Outdoor Venue. Theatre of the Year. Arena/Auditorium of the Year. Best Large Outdoor Concert Venue. Best Live Music Club of the Year. Talent Buyer of the Year.* From large amphitheatres and arenas to small clubs, our venues and staff garner industry accolades year after year. View our upcoming shows, buy tickets and register for presales and special offers at www.hob.com.

The Gorge Amphitheatre is located in George, WA and has been voted Best Outdoor Arena several years running.

the visual blues

The House of Blues' walls feature American folk art affectionately referred to as the visual blues. With over a thousand original pieces of folk art, House of Blues houses one of the largest publicly displayed folk art collections in America. Like music, these pieces represent a form of artistic expression available to everyone.

philanthropy

Throughout our support of the International House of Blues Foundation (IHOBF), over 50,000 students and teachers experience the Blues SchoolHouse program in our music halls annually. This program explores the history, music and cultural impact of the blues and related folk art through live music, narration and a guided tour of our folk art collection. The program highlights African American cultural contributions and emphasizes the importance of personal expression. The IHOBF is dedicated to promoting cultural understanding and creative expression through music and art (www.ihobf.org).

Backing Track List & Index

All tracks are available from the *Lesson Support* site at www.rockhousemethod.com. See page 6 for details.

Blues Guitar - CD 1

BD = Bass and Drums on the track
BDR = Bass, Drums and Rhythm Guitar on the track
BDRL = Bass, Drums, Rhythm Guitar and Lead on the track

1) Introduction
2) Tuning 9
3) Parts of the Guitar 10
4) Reading a Chord Chart 11
5) Open Major Chords 12
6) Open Minor Chords 14
7) Major Blues 16
8) Minor Blues 17
9) Major & Minor Blues *BDR* 17
10) Major & Minor Blues *BD* 17
11) Blues 20
12) Blues *BDR* 20
13) Blues *BD* 20
14) 1st Position A Minor Pentatonic Scale 22
15) 2nd Position A Minor Pentatonic Scale ... 22
16) 3rd Position A Minor Pentatonic Scale ... 23
17) 4th Position A Minor Pentatonic Scale ... 23
18) 5th Position A Minor Pentatonic Scale ... 23
19) Double Lead Pattern (1st Position) 25
20) Double Lead Pattern (2nd Position) 25
21) Triplet Lead Pattern (1st Position) 26
22) Triplet Lead Pattern (2nd Position) 26
23) Lead Techniques - Bending 28
24) Lead Techniques - Hammer Ons 29
25) Lead Techniques - Pull Offs 29
26) Complete Blues Lead 30
27) Complete Blues Lead *BDRL* 30
28) Complete Blues Lead *BDR* 30
29) Blues Riffs - Riff #1 32
30) Blues Riffs - Riff #2 32
31) Blues Riffs - Riff #3 32
32) Blues Riffs - Riff #4 33
33) Blues Riffs - Riff #5 33
34) The B.B. Box 34
35) Shuffle Blues Rhythm 35
36) Shuffle Blues Rhythm *BDR* 35
37) Shuffle Blues Rhythm *BD* 35
38) Full Blues Lead 36
39) Full Blues Lead *BDRL* 36
40) Full Blues Lead *BDR* 36
41) F Major Barre Chord 38
42) F Minor Barre Chord 39
43) F7 Barre Chord 39
44) B♭ Major Barre Chord 40
45) B♭ Minor Barre Chord 41
46) B♭7 Barre Chord 41
47) 12 Bar Blues Progression 42
48) 12 Bar Blues Progression *BDR* 42
49) 12 Bar Blues Progression *BD* 42
50) Single Note Blues Rhythm 43
51) Single Note Blues Rhythm *BDR* 43
52) Single Note Blues Rhythm *BD* 43
53) Lead Techniques - Slides 45
54) Lead Techniques - Vibrato 45
55) Rockin' the Blues 46
56) Rockin' the Blues *BDR* 46
57) Rockin' the Blues *BD* 46
58) Blues Riffs Part 2 - Riff #1 46
59) Blues Riffs Part 2 - Riff #2 47
60) Blues Riffs Part 2 - Riff #3 47
61) Blues Riffs Part 2 - Riff #4 47
62) Blues Riffs Part 2 - Riff #5 47
63) Blues Riffs Part 2 - Riff #6 47
64) Open Chord Blues Progression in Em ... 48
65) Open Chord Blues Progression in Em *BDR* 48
66) Open Chord Blues Progression in Em *BD* 48
67) Blues Scales - Key of E 50
68) Open String Blues Rhythm in E 53
69) Open String Blues Rhythm in E *BDR* ... 53
70) Open String Blues Rhythm in E *BD* 53
71) Advanced Bending Techniques 54
72) Blues Lead in E 55
73) Blues Lead in E *BDRL* 55
74) Blues Lead in E *BDR* 55

Music Minus One Backing Tracks

75) Basic Blues Rhythm (Key of A) *BD*
76) Open Chord Blues Progression (Key of E) *BD*
77) Rockin' the Blues (Key of A) *BD*
78) Single Note Riff Rhythm (Key of D) *BD*
79) Open String Blues Rhythm (Key of E) *BD*

Blues Guitar - CD 2

1) Introduction
2) Tuning
3) A9 Chord 57
4) D9 Chord 57
5) Am7 Chord 58
6) Dm7 Chord 58
7) Amaj7 Chord 59
8) Dmaj7 Chord 59
9) The Jazz Blues Fuze 60
10) The Jazz Blues Fuze *BDR* 60
11) The Jazz Blues Fuze *BD* 60
12) Lead Techniques - Rakes 61
13) Lead Techniques - Pick & Finger 62
14) Advanced Blues Riffs - Riff #1 63
15) Advanced Blues Riffs - Riff #2 63
16) Advanced Blues Riffs - Riff #3 64
17) Advanced Blues Riffs - Riff #4 64
18) Advanced Blues Riffs - Riff #5 64
19) Skipping Strings 67
20) 1st Position C Major Pentatonic Scale 68
21) 2nd Position C Major Pentatonic Scale 68
22) 3rd Position C Major Pentatonic Scale 69
23) 4th Position C Major Pentatonic Scale 69
24) 5th Position C Major Pentatonic Scale 69
25) Fast Blues in C (Sliding Rhythm) 70
26) Fast Blues in C (Sliding Rhythm) *BDR* ... 70
27) Fast Blues in C (Sliding Rhythm) *BD* 70
28) Improvisation Exercise 73
29) Sixteenth Note Lead Pattern 74
30) Blues Rock Progression 76
31) Blues Rock Progression *BDR* 76
32) Blues Rock Progression *BD* 76
33) Classic Old School Blues Turnarounds 78
34) Modern Blues Progression 80
35) Modern Blues Progression *BDR* 80
36) Modern Blues Progression *BD* 80
37) 1st Position A Minor Scale 81
38) 2nd Position A Minor Scale 81
39) Melodic Lead *BDRL* 82
40) Melodic Lead *BDRL slow* 82
41) Slide Technique Rhythm 83
42) Slide Technique Rhythm *BDR* 83
43) Slide Technique Rhythm *BD* 83
44) E Blues Riff Rhythm 84
45) E Blues Riff Rhythm *BDR* 84
46) E Blues Riff Rhythm *BD* 84
47) E Blues Solo *BDRL* 85
48) E Blues Solo *BDRL slow* 85
49) Never Coming Back 87
50) Never Coming Back (excerpt) 87
51) Never Coming Back (excerpt) *slow* 87
52) Conclusion

Music Minus One Backing Tracks

53) Blues Rock Progression (Key of D) *BD*
54) The Jazz Blues Fuze *BD*
55) Modern Blues Progression *BD*
56) Fast Blues in C (Sliding Rhythm) *BD*
57) Slide Technique Rhythm *BD*
58) E Blues Riff Rhythm *BD*